Never Ask Delilah for a Trim...
and other good advice

Never Ask Delilah
for a Trim...
and other good advice

▲ ▼ ▲

Martha Bolton

VINE
BOOKS

SERVANT PUBLICATIONS
ANN ARBOR, MICHIGAN

Vine Books is an imprint of Servant Publications especially designed to serve evangelical Christians.

Published by Servant Publications
P.O. Box 8617
Ann Arbor, Michigan 48107

Cover illustration: Pat Binder
Cover design: PAZ Design Group, Salem, OR

98 99 00 01 10 9 8 7 6 5 4 3 2 1

Printed in the United States of America
ISBN 1-56955-048-4

Library of Congress Cataloging-in-Publication Data

Bolton, Martha, 1951–
    Never ask Delilah for a trim : and other good advice / by Martha Bolton.
        p.   cm.
    Summary: A three-month devotional based on the Gospel of Matthew, providing for each day a short devotion, thoughts to ponder, a Bumper Sticker for the Day, a Scripture to Stand On, and a brief prayer.
    ISBN 1-56955-048-4 (alk. paper)
    1. Teenagers—Prayer-books and devotions—English. 2. Devotional calendars—Juvenile literature. [1. Prayer books and devotions. 2. Devotional calendars.]   I. Title.
    BV4850.B635   1998
    242'.63—dc21   98-8573
                                                           CIP
                                                           AC

Dedication

▲ ▼ ▲

To my niece, Lisa.
May you never forget your worth.

Contents

Acknowledgments

▲ ▼ ▲

A special thank-you to:

My husband, Russ, who recently rigged our kitchen
smoke alarm to play "Come and Dine."

Russ II, Matt, Nicole, Tony, and Kiana, for never refusing a
home-cooked meal, no matter how long it's been smoldering.

My editor, Heidi Hess, for her gentle spirit
and everlasting patience.

And all the youth who have written, faxed, or e-mailed me
(and you both know who you are), I sincerely say,
"Thanks! You're a blessing to my life!"

Foreword

▲ ▼ ▲

The Gospel of Matthew is rich with advice on how we should live our lives. Matthew covers it all: Jesus' Sermon on the Mount, his many parables, our Lord's final week on earth, even end-time prophecies. This three-month devotional is based on Matthew's Gospel.

As with its predecessor, *If the Pasta Wiggles, Don't Eat It ... and other good advice,* this book features ninety short devotions, each requiring only a few minutes to read. There are questions to ponder at the end of each chapter, as well as a Bumper Sticker for the Day, a Scripture to Stand On, and a brief prayer.

It is my sincere hope and prayer that you enjoy this devotional, learn from it, and even have a few laughs along the way. So grab a bag of chips and curl up with *Never Ask Delilah for a Trim....* Just try not to get any salsa on it.

One

▲▼▲

Blessed Are the Tidy...
for Their Clutter Shall Not
Reach the Ceiling

OK, so it's not really a Beatitude, but it is good advice—especially if you're the type of person who hates to throw things away. Like me. I don't throw *anything* out. For years my family thought mold was a frosting. And I can't tell you how often I've had to slice milk from the carton or slip into a toxic-waste suit just to open a quart of cottage cheese.

I'm trying to do better, though. I've vowed to recycle at least ten pieces of paper every day. Is that something you should consider? If you can answer "Yes!" to any of the following questions, it may be a sign that you should think about cleaning up your room, too!

Is your room so cluttered that the spiders are sharing webs?

Is mildew the accent color in your bedroom?

Are there enough recyclable soda cans under your bed to put yourself through college?

Has an exterminator company ever asked to use your bedroom for their training maneuvers?

If you answered yes to any of these, maybe it's time to mow that Chia Bed of yours and cut through the rain forest growing in your closet. Hang up those clothes on something other than the doorknob, like maybe a hanger. And how about erasing those phone messages written in the dust on your desk with a bit of Pledge (after you've copied all the numbers into your address book, of course)?

Who knows what treasures you might find when you really start excavating. But if I were you, I'd warn your parents first. Sometimes adult hearts aren't capable of withstanding that kind of shock!

Thoughts to Ponder:
What does your room say about who you are on the inside?

What are the benefits of a clean room?

Bumper Sticker for the Day:

Man may have been made from dust, but he shouldn't live in it.

Scripture to Stand On:
"With God all things are possible."   MATTHEW 19:26

Hello Again, Lord ...
Lord, help me to keep both my room and my heart free of garbage.

Two

▲ ▼ ▲

Shortcuts

One afternoon while my son Matt was driving in downtown Los Angeles, he found himself stuck in bumper-to-bumper traffic. In an attempt to find a shortcut to his destination and bypass the congestion, he turned onto a seemingly deserted side street. There were a couple of orange barriers partially blocking the access, but he figured that they'd been left behind by some road construction workers, and went around them.

At first it seemed like a good move. There weren't any other vehicles on the street and he was making terrific time. Soon, though, Matt found himself dodging cars coming at him from all directions! It was like the Indy 500 in fast forward. He swerved to the left to miss one. He pulled to the right to miss another. He even got cut off by a taxi with New York plates, which he thought was a little weird, but in Los Angeles anything is possible.

Just then he heard someone yell, "Cut!" A man motioned him over and asked, "Are you an extra?"

My son's "shortcut" had accidentally landed him right in the middle of a movie set!

Taking shortcuts in life can take us where we don't want to be, too. Some people take shortcuts with their education. They try to find an easy way to pass a test or turn in a term paper without really having to work at it. Others will take shortcuts with their families, their job, even with God. But more often than not, shortcuts only shortchange us.

Thoughts to Ponder:

Have you been taking shortcuts lately? Can you think of a time when a "shorter" or "easier" way turned out to be just the opposite?

What can you do to keep from making the same mistake again?

Bumper Sticker for the Day:

> **Many a shortcut has
> ended up a deadend.**

Scripture to Stand On:

"Again, the kingdom of heaven is like a merchant looking for fine pearls. When he found one of great value, he went away and sold everything he had and bought it."

MATTHEW 13:45-46

Hello Again, Lord ...

Lord, remind me that when I give all I've got to you, I get all you've got in return.

Three

▲▼▲

Convenient Faith

Do you know someone who uses the Lord? You know, the type of person who thinks it's OK to ride in the carpool lane because "Jesus is with me." People like this slap bumper stickers all over their cars, desks, and lockers. But the minute their testimony begins to hinder their standing with the "cool" crowd, it gets hidden faster than a Hershey bar at a Weight Watchers' meeting.

"Convenience Christians" try to have it both ways. They sport a fish decal on their T-shirt, but handle relationships like a barracuda. They don't see anything wrong with quoting all the Beatitudes in Sunday school class, then "sharing" the latest off-color joke at school on Monday. Their version of the twenty-third Psalm would begin like this: "The Lord is my shepherd, but I shall not want him interfering with my life every day."

This kind of "faith" is not real faith at all. We all make mistakes sometimes, but faith isn't something we put on and take off, like gym clothes. If we truly love God, our faith is part of who we are, twenty-four hours a day, 7 days a week, 365 days a year.

Thoughts to Ponder:

Are there any ways in which you think you might be "using" God?

How do you think God feels when we "use" him?

Bumper Sticker for the Day:

> **Your testimony should stick longer than your bumper sticker.**

Scripture to Stand On:

"These people honor me with their lips, but their hearts are far from me."

MATTHEW 15:8

Hello Again, Lord ...

Lord, help my faith to be real, not just convenient.

Four

▲▼▲

Hey, Don't Blame the Mailman!

Picture this: Your best friend does something to hurt you. You're so offended that you immediately sit down and write a letter telling her off. You get everything off your chest, even bring up a number of her past offenses (you've been saving them all on your computer anyway). Satisfied, you rush out and mail the letter.

The next day your "former" best friend says that she feels bad about what happened, and apologizes to you. Of course, you say that you understand and forgive her. You even say you're sorry back, for having doubted her friendship. You both vow to let *nothing* ever come between you again ... that is, until you remember (gulp!) *the letter!*

There's no way to retrieve it now. You can't go back to that mailbox, reach in, and start pulling out letters until you find yours (that's a federal offense). You can't hide out at your friend's house and tackle her letter carrier as he makes his delivery (that's an even greater federal offense). No, that letter's destined to be delivered, and there's not a thing you can do to stop it.

When we're feeling angry or hurt, our first instinct is often to even up the score, right then and there. The smart thing to do, though, is to allow things to simmer down. If we take our time responding and make decisions with a clear head, instead of in the heat of the moment, we'll have fewer regrets later on.

It's quite possible that after thinking and praying about it, we still may need to confront someone who's hurt us. But then we can do it calmly, in a spirit of love and genuine concern, and not out of anger or retaliation. That's the best way anyway, because words spoken or written in a loving spirit seldom have to be taken back.

Thoughts to Ponder:

When was the last time you wished you could take back something you had said or done?

What do you wish you had said or done instead? What can you learn from this experience?

Bumper Sticker for the Day:

> ### God's diet plan:
> ### Reduce the number of words
> ### you have to eat each day.

Scripture to Stand On:

"But I tell you that anyone who is angry with his brother will be subject to judgment."

MATTHEW 5:22

Hello Again, Lord ...

Lord, help me to remember it's better to think about my actions before I do them than to spend the rest of my life regretting them.

Five
▲▼▲

Makin' History

Do you know there are some talented people that you'll never read about in your history books?

Michaelangelo's twin brother started a mural on his bedroom ceiling, but quit because no one would hold the ladder for him.

Leonardo da Vinci's neighbor was the first to promise Mona Lisa that he'd paint her portrait, but somehow he never got around to picking up a new set of oils from the art supply store.

Shakespeare's stepsister thought about writing a play, but used up all her ink just doodling with her quill pen.

Beethoven's second cousin could actually compose better symphonies than Beethoven. But he was so fearful that someone would steal them, he just hummed them all in his head.

Amelia Earhart's best friend wanted to be a pilot, but never got around to signing up for that "Fear of Flying" class.

Steven Spielberg's gardener wanted to make blockbuster movies, but figured all the good ideas had already been taken.

Billy Graham's barber felt called to be an evangelist, but could never conquer his stage fright.

Mother Teresa's friend considered giving her life to God's work, too, but decided to spend her years seeking fame and admiration instead. She found neither. Mother Teresa got both.

Obviously, these "nearly famous" people are fictitious, but you get my point. It takes more than talent to make history.

Thoughts to Ponder:

What excuses have you used to keep from using the talents God has given you?

Why do you think God wants us to use our talents for him?

Bumper Sticker for the Day:

Talents aren't like merchandise. You don't get credit for returning them unused.

Scripture to Stand On:

"His master replied, 'Well done, good and faithful servant! You have been faithful with a few things; I will put you in charge of many things. Come and share your master's happiness!'"

MATTHEW 25:23

Hello Again, Lord ...

Remind me, Lord, that the gifts you've given me were intended to be shared with others.

Six

▲▼▲

Who Ya Gonna Call?

One of the most important telephone numbers you will ever learn is "911." Each year thousands of lives are saved because someone knew how to dial that number.

Not every call that comes in to the 911 line is an emergency, however. There are those who have called it for weather reports, traffic updates, or to find out how long to cook a pork roast. They're not supposed to do this, of course—"911" is for life-or-death situations only. If you dial it to order one of my recipes, they'll probably disconnect you (even though some of my recipes *do* represent a life-or-death situation).

There's another number you need to know how to call in emergencies, too. God's number. It's not 911. In fact, you don't even have to dial a number at all. It's an automatic connection as soon as you call on his name. God's line is open twenty-four hours a day, and it can handle all of life's problems, from life-threatening emergencies to everyday concerns.

So the next time you're in need of some divine "emergency assistance," the next time you have some emotional cuts or bruises that need to be attended to STAT, who ya gonna call?

Thoughts to Ponder:

Who do you call on first when you're faced with a crisis in your life?

Why do you think God cares just as much about our small problems as he does our big ones?

Bumper Sticker for the Day:

> **God handles billions of calls a day, and he's never hung up on anyone.**

Scripture to Stand On:

"If you believe, you will receive whatever you ask for in prayer."

MATTHEW 21:22

Hello Again, Lord ...

Lord, thank you for always being there in my time of need. And all the other times, too.

Seven

▲▼▲

Don't Rush It!

In high school, I was on a bowling league. I loved to bowl. At one point in my life, I even thought about becoming a professional bowler. Not that I was good enough, but it would have been fun to try.

There was only one thing about bowling that I didn't like (besides the shoes, I mean). I hated waiting for my ball to return between rolls. It seemed to take forever, and there was nothing to do but stand there and hold my hand over the hand blower and wait. And wait. And wait.

One day I got a great idea. I'd save three or four seconds, I figured, if I helped the ball along a little bit. I'd just put my hand down the mouth of the ball chute and grab the ball as soon as it got close enough to the opening. The minute I stretched my arm into the dark, circular hole, however, I realized that I'd made a huge mistake.

I tried removing my hand, but it was too late. The force of the conveyor belt kept pushing that ten-pound ball against my hand, and there was no way to free myself. Needless to say, there was a lot of pain and screaming involved. Finally, a teammate ran and told the manager to turn off the ball return.

Thankfully, I didn't have any broken bones, and it only took about a week for the swelling and discoloration to go away. My bruised ego took a little longer to heal.

As Christians, we are sometimes impatient in waiting for God to respond to our requests. We want to hurry the answers along, but more often than not, we just get in the way, plugging up the flow of God's blessings in our lives.

We must learn to relax, trusting that the answers to our prayers are going to come in God's perfect time. Not a second too early. Not a second too late.

Thoughts to Ponder:

Are you growing impatient, wondering if God is ever going to answer a prayer of yours?

Why do you think it's important to trust God's timing?

Bumper Sticker for the Day:

God's clock has perfect timing.
Don't try to reset it.

Scripture to Stand On:

"Your kingdom come, your will be done, on earth as it is in heaven."

MATTHEW 6:10

Hello Again, Lord ...

Lord, give me the patience to wait for your perfect timing in my life.

Eight

▲▼▲

House Pets

I recently read a newspaper article about a pet boa constrictor that squeezed the life out of its teenage owner. The boy's parents were distraught and lamented to the reporter, "We trusted that snake."

It's sad that boy lost his life, but as well as he thought he knew his pet, there came a point when he stopped being in control and that snake started calling all the shots.

How many times do we do that ourselves? How often do we allow something harmful into our lives—bad habits, poor judgments, compromising actions, undesirable friends—and refuse to let go of these things until we are caught in sin's deadly "squeeze"? What do you think God will say when we cry, "but I trusted that snake!"

Now don't get me wrong. I'm not saying you shouldn't have a pet snake. (I prefer house pets with tails that wag instead of squeeze, but that's me.) If you do own a snake, though, you know it's important to use wisdom in handling them. A snake can turn on you in an instant.

Life's "snakes" almost always will.

Thoughts to Ponder:

What kind of "snakes" are you trusting?

Why do you think God warns us about letting sin into our lives?

Bumper Sticker for the Day:

Scripture to Stand On:

"Enter through the narrow gate. For wide is the gate, and broad is the road that leads to destruction, and many enter through it."

MATTHEW 7:13

Hello Again, Lord ...

Lord, help me to remember that in you alone I should place my trust.

Nine

▲▼▲

Turning Corners

My father was a carpenter, a very good carpenter. No matter what you needed built or repaired, he was the one who could do it.

In high school, my sister and I asked him to make a float for a parade our school was having. Dad worked on it all day long and did a wonderful job. The float had a flat bed to sit on, huge wheels that rolled with ease, and a wooden bar in front to pull it along the parade route.

There was only one problem. We forgot to tell Dad that the float was going to have to turn corners. The wheels didn't have axles, and every time we came to a curve in the path, we all had to get down and push or pull the float to the left or to the right (in mermaid costumes, no less). We were, I'm sure, the most noticeable float in the parade, but not for the reasons we'd hoped.

Some of us are like that float. We're fine as long as everything is moving along in a straight line. But let life throw us a curve and we can't handle it. We end up stranded by the side of the road, or worse yet, off in a ditch somewhere, trying to figure out how we got there and how we can get back in the parade.

Thoughts to Ponder:

What is the latest "curve" life has thrown you?

Why do you think it's important to be able to adjust to unexpected changes in our lives?

Bumper Sticker for the Day:

> **People, like cars,
> last a lot longer when they
> can handle the turns in the road.**

Scripture to Stand On:

"Who of you by worrying can add a single hour to his life?"

MATTHEW 6:27

Hello Again, Lord ...

Lord, whenever life throws me a curve, I'm glad that you're there to help straighten it out.

Ten

▲▼▲

That's MY Moses
You're Talking About

Did you know that Moses' brother, Aaron, and his sister, Miriam, talked about him behind his back? Here was a man with whom God spoke face to face. The Bible even calls him the meekest man in all the earth, and still his siblings bad-mouthed him.

Sometimes when you're doing a good thing, those closest to you get jealous. They backbite. They criticize. They may even spread untruths about you. But Moses left his reputation in God's hands. He didn't have to defend himself because God did it for him. That's right. God. The Creator of the Universe, the Omnipotent One, the great I Am spoke up for Moses. How's that for a character witness?

God himself confronted Miriam and Aaron about what they had done. He cross-examined them, and the truth prevailed. Miriam even came down with a bad case of seven-day leprosy. (God healed her after seven days for Moses' sake.)

So, if you have a friend, family member, or an enemy who's backbiting, gossiping, or falsely accusing you, leave it in God's hands. I'm not saying he'll zap that person with leprosy (you wouldn't really want that anyway), but he has an excellent track record of standing up for his faithful. And with him in your corner, who else do you need?

Thoughts to Ponder:

Have you ever been falsely accused of something? How did it make you feel?

What do you think makes a person backbite?

Bumper Sticker for the Day:

> **The Father, Son, and Holy Ghost—the best defense team around.**

Scripture to Stand On:

"Blessed are you when people insult you, persecute you and falsely say all kinds of evil against you because of me."

MATTHEW 5:11

Hello Again, Lord ...

Lord, help me to know when to speak up in my defense, and when to be quiet and give you the floor.

Eleven

▲▼▲

Acting a Little Squirrelly?

Why did the chicken cross the road? To show the squirrel how it's done. Squirrels don't have a clue as to how to cross a street. Oh, they'll try, but more often than not, they end up as someone's hood ornament. The problem? Indecision.

When no traffic's coming, a squirrel stays calmly and safely on the curb. But let a few cars and diesel trucks come zooming down the road, and the daring little creature darts right into their path. When he hears the traffic screech to a stop, he just stares innocently into the headlights as if to say, "What'd you expect me to do? Use the crosswalk? I'm a *squirrel.* I can't read."

Tail dragging between his legs, Mr. Squirrel heads back to the curb. Then, when all the drivers think it's safe to proceed again, that fickle critter tries it one more time. He scurries back across the street. Boom. Squirrel pancake.

Indecision is different than caution. Caution is that little voice inside you that tells you not to go scuba diving in a shark tank just before feeding time. Caution keeps you from practicing your electric guitar in the shower, and warns you not to sample my tofu and liver casserole without plenty of antacids on hand.

Indecision, on the other hand, can be dangerous. It usually stems from fear, not wisdom. Indecision gives us cold feet when we should have courage, and doubts when we should have determination. Indecision can make us miss out on many of the opportunities and blessings that God has intended for us.

So whenever you have an important decision to make, pray about it, get good counsel from your parents or some other adult whose judgment you trust, then make your decision. Don't be like that squirrel who made a decision, then kept changing his mind again and again and again, until that decision became his last.

Thoughts to Ponder:

Do you have a decision you're struggling with?

What things could you do that would help you come to a decision?

Bumper Sticker for the Day:

> ### Not making a decision
> ### is making a decision.

Scripture to Stand On:

"No one can serve two masters. Either he will hate the one and love the other, or he will be devoted to the one and despise the other."

MATTHEW 6:24

Hello Again, Lord ...

Lord, may I always make the right decisions and have the courage to stand by them.

Twelve

▲▼▲

Forgiveness Is a
Two-Way Street

There was once a man who owed a king a huge sum of money (see Mt 18:23-35). Evidently, he had maxed out on all his credit cards big time, so the king commanded that the man's family and all that he owned be sold to pay the debt.

"Pleeeeeeease," the man begged. "Give me a little more time. I'll get an advance on my Visa account. I'll cash in all my aluminum cans. I'll have a garage sale. I just need some more time to get the money. Trust me." Or words to that effect.

Now, the king could have demanded interest-only payments. He could have made the man walk the royal dog for the next twenty years to work off his debt. But that's not what happened.

Instead, the king forgave this man's entire bill! All 10,000 talents of it (something MasterCard or Visa would never do)! The king wiped the slate clean, stamped "Paid in Full" right on his monthly statement.

Now, you'd think this man would be so appreciative that he'd pass along the kindness to someone else, right? But noooo... The Bible says that the forgiven man went out and found another man, one who owed him a much smaller amount than the one he had owed the king (sort of like a library fine compared to the national debt). When the second poor man couldn't pay, the first man had him thrown into debtor's prison.

How often do we see this same behavior in other Christians? How about (gulp) in your own life? When a Christian brother or sister slips up, do you want to throw the book at that person? Or do you remember all the times you have sinned, all the times God has forgiven (and continues to forgive) you? If we keep in mind our own shortcomings, it's much easier to show God's mercy to those who need it most.

Thoughts to Ponder:

What do you think Jesus wanted to teach us through the Parable of the Unmerciful Servant?

Is there someone in your life to whom you could show mercy today?

Bumper Sticker for the Day:

> ### A forgiven Christian is a forgiving Christian.

Scripture to Stand On:

"Shouldn't you have had mercy on your fellow servant just as I had on you?"

MATTHEW 18:33

Hello Again, Lord ...

Lord, help me to remember my sins long enough to forget my brother's.

Thirteen
▲▼▲

What a Friend

Throughout life, we'll have many different kinds of friends. Some will be "good time" friends. These are the ones who'll stay right by our side as long as we're having fun, but the minute things get a little tough, their loyalty fizzles. (Sort of like Peter's did the night before Jesus was crucified.)

Then there are the "what's in it for me" kind of friends. They're committed to the friendship as long as it's in their favor. Like an insurance company, when the benefits run out, they drop you.

How do you recognize true friends?

A true friend will find something positive to say about your new permanent, even though it looks like you bathed with the toaster.

A true friend is someone who puts a rubber snake in your sleeping bag at camp, then warns you about it.

A true friend can see you at your worst and not take pictures.

You can confide in a true friend ... and rest assured that she won't confide your secret in six hundred of *her* closest friends.

A true friend will never walk out on you, even after you've shown her the door.

A true friend lets you vent, even though all that's coming out is hot air.

A true friend believes the best about you, even when everyone else is pointing to the worst.

A true friend knows you well enough to hug you when you yourself don't even realize you need it.

But for me, the real mark of a true friend is someone who, when I invite them over for a home-cooked meal, asks for seconds!

Thoughts to Ponder:

Who in your life is a true friend?

What kind of a friend are you to others?

Bumper Sticker for the Day:

A true friend sticks closer than a brother. A false friend just sticks it to you.

Scripture to Stand On:

"Love your neighbor as yourself."

MATTHEW 19:19

Hello Again, Lord ...

Lord, help me to be the kind of friend to others that you are to me.

Fourteen

▲▼▲

I Wanna Thank
All the Little People

Do you know how many seemingly insignificant people God has used throughout history to do remarkable things?

The Bible doesn't mention the name of the young boy with the five loaves and two fishes (see Jn 6:1-14), but he was clearly the smartest person in the crowd (besides Jesus, that is) because he was the only one who brought a lunch. His willingness to share what little he had was used by our Lord to perform one of the greatest miracles in the Bible.

David was pretty insignificant, too, a mere shepherd boy going up against the giant, Goliath. This was in the days before tag teams. Hulk Hogan couldn't step in and take David's place when things started looking a little grim. David had to face Goliath by himself, but he knew that God was on his side. Using his slingshot, David hit Goliath square between the eyes, knocking him out cold and scoring yet another win for "the little guy."

Mary was just a young girl living in an insignificant little town called Nazareth. She probably wasn't on the honor roll or on the Nazareth High School cheerleading team. She was what some might call a "nobody." But God didn't think of her as a nobody. He chose her to be the mother of the greatest Somebody who ever lived.

So if you're feeling inadequate, insignificant, or outnumbered today, just remember, the smaller we are (especially when it comes to our egos), the more God can use us.

Thoughts to Ponder:

Can you remember a time when you felt insignificant or overwhelmed? Tell about it.

Why do you think God repeatedly chooses the "little" or seemingly insignificant guy or gal to do his greatest works?

Bumper Sticker for the Day:

If God had a bumper sticker,
it'd say, "All my children
are honor students."

Scripture to Stand On:

"Blessed are the meek, for they will inherit the earth."

MATTHEW 5:5

Hello Again, Lord ...

Lord, help me to believe in myself as much as you believe in me.

Fifteen

▲ ▼ ▲

Running

 ver feel like running away? When things get tough,
it's tempting to escape, to run from problems, hurts,
people, and fears.

I almost ran away from home once, but I only made it as
far as our front porch, got scared, then stood there waiting
to see if anyone would come after me. My mother did, of
course, and we both had a good laugh when she opened the
door and saw me standing there. Today, I don't even
remember what I was running from, but I'm glad the front
porch was as far as I got.

The Bible tells us that Jonah tried running away, too.
From God. God told him to go to Nineveh and preach to
the people there. But Jonah had other career plans, and
boarded a ship headed for Tarshish instead.

As soon as Jonah set off in the wrong direction, away
from God, his troubles began. A violent storm hit, and the
other passengers found out who he was running away from
and threw him overboard. God didn't let him drown,
though. He sent along a big fish to swallow him whole, and
kept Jonah there for the next three days. Not exactly the
Hilton, but it did give Jonah a chance to think about his dis-
obedience.

When Jonah decided to quit running and to obey God
instead, things took a turn for the better. The fish spit him

out onto dry ground, Jonah went on to Nineveh and preached there, and the entire city repented and turned back to God! Jonah found out the task God was asking him to do wasn't nearly as difficult as he feared.

So you see, running away is never the answer. It doesn't solve our troubles, it just postpones our dealing with them. As in Jonah's case, it may even increase them. If we take off every time a problem arises in our lives, all we're going to do is end up an awful long way from home and from God's will.

Thoughts to Ponder:

Have you ever felt like running away? Why?

Why do you think it's better to stay and face your problems?

Bumper Sticker for the Day:

> **Running from problems
> is never the answer to them.**

Scripture to Stand On:

He replied, "You of little faith, why are you so afraid?" Then he got up and rebuked the winds and the waves, and it was completely calm.

MATTHEW 8:26

Hello Again, Lord ...

Lord, whenever I feel like running, may it always be to you.

Sixteen
▲▼▲

Picky, Picky, Picky

Do you have overly critical people in your life? People who find something wrong with everyone and everything around them? They visit Mount Rushmore and all they see is the bush growing out of Lincoln's nose. They gaze upon the Mona Lisa and wonder why someone doesn't give her an updated hairstyle. They go to Niagara Falls and complain because no one's made a water park out of it yet.

Complain, complain, complain.

If they were with Joshua when God caused the walls of Jericho to fall down, they would have whined, "All this dust is going to be murder on my asthma!" Had they been with Moses at the parting of the Red Sea, they would have said, "This is nice, but couldn't God have been a bit more creative and zigzagged it or something?"

The biggest problem with critical people is that they hate suffering alone. They feel lousy and they'll do their best to make you feel lousy, too. But don't let them get the best of you. Keep yourself focused on uplifting things and surround yourself with positive people. After all, you only get one chance to weave the tapestry of your life. Don't miss all its beauty by hanging around the moths.

Thoughts to Ponder:

Why do you think some people tend to look on the negative side of things?

If you have a negative person in your life, what can you do to help that person start thinking more positively?

Bumper Sticker for the Day:

> **Negative (-) people
> subtract from your joy.
> Positive (+) people
> add to it.**

Scripture to Stand On:

"Therefore do not worry about tomorrow, for tomorrow will worry about itself. Each day has enough trouble of its own."

MATTHEW 6:34

Hello Again, Lord ...

Lord, help me to see the beauty of the flowers, instead of always dwelling on the compost.

Seventeen

▲▼▲

Self-Defense Prayer

One of the hardest Scriptures to follow is Matthew 5:44. It's the part of Jesus' Sermon on the Mount where he tells us how to handle our enemies. He doesn't advise us to take an advanced self-assertiveness class or primal scream therapy. Jesus suggests a better way to handle our enemies. He tells us to pray for them.

It's a tough Scripture to follow. On the surface, it doesn't seem fair. After all, why should someone who has hurt us get let off the hook so easily? What good does it do if all they get for the grief they have given us is … our prayers?

Believe it or not, praying for our enemies is the best thing we can do for *ourselves*. There's plenty of medical evidence proving that hanging on to ill feelings can be hazardous to our health. Depression, headaches, ulcers, stomach problems, high blood pressure … often these ailments can be traced to an unforgiving heart.

So, when Jesus tells us to pray for our enemies, to bless those who curse us, it's out of love for *us*. And besides, when we start praying for them, who knows—they just might change, the situation might change, and we might even change a little, too.

Thoughts to Ponder:

Why do you suppose that Jesus said, "Pray for your enemies," instead of "Follow me and you will not *have* enemies"?

What kinds of things do you think can happen in our own lives when we start praying for our enemies?

Bumper Sticker for the Day:

> ### The best way to bring an enemy to his knees is to start there ourselves.

Scripture to Stand On:

"But I tell you: Love your enemies and pray for those who persecute you, that you may be sons of your Father in heaven."

MATTHEW 5:44-45

Hello Again, Lord ...

Lord, help me to spend more time praying for my enemies and less time complaining about them.

Eighteen

▲▼▲

Credit Where Credit Is Due

Imagine yourself as the director of a movie. You dedicate yourself to it and pour your undivided attention into it for months, maybe even years. You stay awake nights just thinking about every aspect of it. You're so proud of your "baby," you could bust!

Now, imagine watching the credits roll at the premiere screening, and noticing that under the words "Directed by ..." it's blank! Your name isn't listed! Or worse yet, what if an actor's name was listed as the director? How would that make you feel? Not very good, would it?

Sometimes, when we have the opportunity to give credit where credit is due, we make no mention of the Lord and his direction in our lives. Perhaps we even fool ourselves into thinking that it was our own talents and skills, or even our own wisdom, that brought us whatever success we enjoy. We either leave the "Directed by ..." line blank, or we place our own names there and selfishly accept all the praise rightfully due him.

But that's not how it's supposed to be. When God leads and guides our lives, he deserves the director's credit. We need to make sure he gets it.

Thoughts to Ponder:

Why do you think it's important to give God credit for the good things that have happened in our lives?

In what ways can we give God credit for guiding our lives?

Bumper Sticker for the Day:

> ### The creation should never upstage the Creator.

Scripture to Stand On:

"In the same way, let your light shine before men, that they may see your good deeds and praise your Father in heaven."

MATTHEW 5:16

Hello Again, Lord ...

Lord, may I never fail to give you the credit for directing my life.

Nineteen

▲ ▼ ▲

Unspoken Words

One evening, entertainer Mark Lowry called to tell me how much he appreciated me and my work. That night a friend of his, Rich Mullins, had been tragically killed in a traffic accident.

Rich's death came so suddenly that Mark regretted not having had more time to learn from him, talk with him, and share with him how much he admired his life and talent. So, Mark wasn't taking any more chances. He didn't want anyone else leaving this world without hearing the things he wanted to say. He was calling every friend and relative in his address book and telling them he loved them. It was already late in the evening, and he had just gotten to the B's.

I admire Mark for taking the time to make those telephone calls. How often do we think about telling our friends and families how much we love and appreciate them? And yet, we never seem to get around to doing it. Or we think we have to wait until we can do something big enough, meaningful enough, or memorable enough ... then end up not doing anything at all.

When my father passed away, I was reminded how very short life is. So I made a vow that I was going to hug my mother and tell her how much I loved her every single time I saw her, which was almost daily. Most of the time she got several hugs in the same visit. Now that she's gone, I can't tell you how glad I am that I made that vow.

It's difficult losing those we love through death. And yet, if we tell them how we feel about them now, it will mean more to them—and to us—than all the tears we shed at their funeral.

Thoughts to Ponder:

Are there people in your life who need to hear what they mean to you? Who are they?

What is it you'd like to say to them?

Bumper Sticker for the Day:

> **The best eulogy
> is one that's not a surprise
> to the deceased.**

Scripture to Stand On:

"Blessed are those who mourn, for they will be comforted."

MATTHEW 5:4

Hello Again, Lord ...

Lord, remind me that the "right moment" to tell someone I care about them is always now.

Twenty
▲▼▲

1-800-He-Knows

The other day I was cut off by the driver of an eighteen-wheeler. I hit my brakes, slid to a screeching stop, and came frighteningly close to slamming into his "How am I driving?" bumper sticker.

Personally, I'd never put one of those stickers on the back of my car. My telephone lines couldn't handle all those incoming calls. I once flunked a driving test because I didn't know the speed limit on a sidewalk. (How was I supposed to know it was a trick question?)

Another time I ran a red light. I was listening to a commercial on the radio, waiting for the light to turn green; when the station resumed playing music, I automatically resumed driving! I was already through the intersection when I finally came to my senses and realized what I had done. Needless to say, I felt pretty stupid.

No, I'd never put a "How Am I Driving?" bumper sticker on my car. And I'd venture to say, most of us wouldn't … at least not voluntarily. We don't want others judging our driving skills that closely.

Most of us don't want others judging our lives that closely either. I sometimes wonder how differently we'd live if we had a sign on our backs that said "How am I living?" with an 800 number people could call to report hearing us lose our temper in a restaurant, or seeing us remain silent when a store clerk undercharged us. If there were a central office that took reports of un-Christlike behavior, how would we act? Chances are we'd behave a lot better if we knew that kind of scrutiny was going on.

But we don't need a number for people to call. All that we do wrong and all that we do right doesn't have to be called in to anyone. God already knows.

Thoughts to Ponder:

Are you the same person when no one's looking as when you know you're being watched? Why or why not?

Why do you think it's important for people to see consistency in our walk with the Lord?

Bumper Sticker for the Day:

Life is like three-way calling. God's always listening in.

Scripture to Stand On:

"But the one who received the seed that fell on good soil is the man who hears the word and understands it. He produces a crop, yielding a hundred, sixty or thirty times what was sown."

MATTHEW 13:23

Hello Again, Lord ...

Lord, help me to remember that my life can be an encouragement to others or a hindrance. It all depends on how I live it.

Twenty-one

▲▼▲

And Now Introducing ...

There are a couple of people I'd like you to get to know better. I'm pretty sure you've already met. You probably even live with one or both of them. They're your parents.

How much do you really know about that woman who, whether she works at home or in the workplace, manages to drive you from soccer practice to piano lessons to swim meets to Friday night football games every week? And what about that man who comes home around the same time every night and sits across the dinner table from you, asking for seconds of the mashed potatoes? (My husband never asks for firsts, but that's a different story.)

Sure, you think you know your parents, but do you really? To find out, see how many of the following questions you can answer correctly:

* When's your mother's birthday? Your father's?

* How did your mother and father meet? Where did they honeymoon?

* What's your dad's favorite color? Your mother's favorite song?

* What's the one thing they've always dreamed of doing?

* Who picked out your name—your mother, your father, or both?

* What was your father's best subject? Your mother's?

* Did either of your parents have a favorite pet when they were growing up? What was its name?

* What was the best prank your father ever played on someone?

* What are your parents' most embarrassing moments? Their favorite memories?

* What is the number one rule they think their parents were right in enforcing?

If you don't know the answers to any of the above questions, go ask your mom or dad. After all, the rule "Never talk to strangers" shouldn't mean your parents.

Thoughts to Ponder:
What one thing about your parents do you find most interesting?

If you could ask your parents any question at all, what would it be?

Bumper Sticker for the Day:

Your parents have a story to tell. You might be the only one privileged to hear it.

Scripture to Stand On:
"For God said, 'Honor your father and mother'"

MATTHEW 15:4

Hello Again, Lord ...
Lord, help me to honor my father and mother with my ears, as well as with my mouth.

Twenty-two

▲ ▼ ▲

Dear Diary

Ever feel sorry for yourself? Who hasn't? Friends can fail us, family members may hurt our feelings or abandon us, or we might suffer unbearable losses. Life can get tough. But before we document those injustices in our diaries, we should take a moment to compare our problems with those faced by others throughout history. The comparison might sound something like this:

"Dear Diary: What a lousy day this has been! First I couldn't get my locker open. Then I tripped and dropped my English homework in a puddle of water. I forgot my lunch money and had to starve until three o'clock! Now my mom tells me that I've got to baby-sit my little brother tonight when I had plans to go skating with my friends. Life just isn't fair!"

Now imagine another diary, written by one of the early Christians, Stephen: "Dear Diary: On the outside it probably looks as if I'm not having a very good day. They say they're going to stone me to death for just sharing the gospel. I don't understand it. You'd think they'd want to hear about God's love. But if death is the price I must pay for following God, then I gladly lay down my life."

A few days later, our diary entry reads: "Dear Diary: My sister wore my sweater *again* without asking. And she didn't wear any deodorant. I know this for a fact because when I hung it back up in my closet, three moths dropped dead!"

Now imagine reading Joseph's diary, just after he was transported to Egypt: "Dear Diary: My brothers threw me in a pit and sold me into slavery. I guess this means I won't be getting a birthday card from them again this year. I only hope that someday I'll be able to repay their jealousy and injustice with kindness and mercy."

As you can see, when we compare our troubles to those faced by Stephen, Joseph, Job, Paul, and others in the Bible who met with seemingly insurmountable problems, our diary entries would then have to read: "Dear Diary: I don't have a single thing to complain about today!"

Thoughts to Ponder:

Name some other people who have already or who might be going through a more difficult trial than what you're facing:

What can you learn from how they handled or are handling their crisis?

Bumper Sticker for the Day:

> **If anyone had a right to complain, it was Jesus. Lucky for us, he didn't.**

Scripture to Stand On:

"Rejoice and be glad, because great is your reward in heaven, for in the same way they persecuted the prophets who were before you."

MATTHEW 5:12

Hello Again, Lord ...

Lord, the next time I start to complain about all my sacrifices, remind me of yours.

Twenty-three
▲▼▲

They Don't Know Who
They're Messin' With

Do you ever find yourself in situations where you wish God would part the Red Sea again, or do something equally spectacular to prove to the world that he is who he says he is? Say you're involved in a spirited discussion with one of your teachers who claims to be an atheist. Wouldn't it be great if God would show his power to your teacher at that very moment? Nothing too showy—maybe a small lightning storm inside the classroom, or perhaps a four-point earthquake centered directly under your teacher's desk.

And when that classmate of yours repeatedly uses the Lord's name in vain, wouldn't it be cool if God would send a swarm of locusts down to eat his science project? Why, you might even be willing to walk around the cafeteria seven times if you knew God would make the walls come a tumblin' down ... especially on Tuna Surprise Day!

We'd love for God to make an unexpected appearance to our skeptical friends and family, maybe even show up on "Larry King Live" or during the halftime show at the Super Bowl. But he doesn't. That doesn't mean he can't. God can prove himself to anyone at any time. But there's more than enough evidence already on record to document God's existence. Maybe he just figures he shouldn't have to keep proving himself to get people to believe.

Thoughts to Ponder:

After all the miracles God has performed since the beginning of time, why do you think some people still refuse to believe?

List the reasons why you know that God is real:

Bumper Sticker for the Day:

An atheist:
Someone who thinks
covering his eyes
will make God go away.

Scripture to Stand On:

"Come follow me," Jesus said, "and I will make you fishers of men."

MATTHEW 4:19

Hello Again, Lord ...

Lord, help me to spend more time introducing you to my friends than I do debating you with them.

Twenty-four

▲▼▲

Hit the Brakes

As I was preparing to back out of the parking lot at our local post office late one afternoon, I shifted my car into "reverse," then inadvertently pressed the gas pedal instead of the brake. Luckily, there weren't any other cars around, so I didn't hit anything. (But I did notice several postmen diving for cover.)

By the time I realized what had happened, my car had executed a complete backward circle. It was pretty embarrassing. I had never done a donut in my life. In fact, the only time I had ever burned rubber was when I had left my son's wet suit in the dryer too long.

I quickly pulled myself together as best I could, carefully shifted the car into "drive," then proceeded home. And other than the two dreams I've had since then of being the lead car in a NASCAR race, I've pretty much put the whole incident behind me.

But I wonder how many of us have done that in life—hit the gas when we should have hit the brakes. We think we know exactly what we are doing and charge full speed ahead. After a few unexpected donuts, though, we suddenly realize that all we're doing is going full speed *backward*.

Thoughts to Ponder:

Looking back on your life, can you think of a time when you "hit the gas" when you should have "hit the brakes" instead? Tell about it:

Why do you think it would have been smarter for you to have hit the brakes?

Bumper Sticker for the Day:

For cars and people,
brakes aren't optional equipment.

Scripture to Stand On:

"This is my blood of the covenant, which is poured out for many for the forgiveness of sins."

MATTHEW 26:28

Hello Again, Lord ...

Lord, help me to apply the brakes before it's too late for them to do me any good.

Twenty-five

▲▼▲

Watch Your Manners

Do you have good manners when it comes to God?

Do you thank him when he blesses you, or do you just accept the blessing and go about your day?

Do you say you're sorry when you've let him down, or do you not say anything, figuring that, since he's God, he should already know how you feel?

When you're praying, do you give him a chance to speak to your heart, or do you monopolize the conversation?

Do you let him walk before you, or are you constantly trying to take cuts, maneuvering yourself into the lead position? Do you go where he wants you to go, or do you take him to places he'd rather not be?

Is he included in your daily plans, or do you routinely leave him out? Do you talk to him on a regular basis, friend to friend, or do you ignore him until you need something?

Funny, isn't it—when it comes to manners, some of us just don't think they apply to God.

Thoughts to Ponder:

Do you think God deserves to be treated with respect and good manners? Why?

What are some ways that we can show better manners to God?

> ## If Jesus didn't care about manners,
> ## he wouldn't have pointed out
> ## the nine unthankful lepers.

Scripture to Stand On:

"At that time Jesus said, 'I praise you, Father, Lord of heaven and earth.'"

MATTHEW 11:25

Hello Again, Lord ...

Lord, help me to remember my manners when it comes to you.

Twenty-six

▲ ▼ ▲

Tongue-Tied

Aren't you glad God knows what we mean to say, even when it doesn't come out quite right?

One Friday night at youth group, my youngest son Tony was asked to pray over the offering. Being a teenager of few words, he walked to the front of the room, bowed his head and said, "Lord bless us as we bring you our thighs."

Once, a preacher I knew was in the middle of a spirited sermon. The church had no air conditioning, and it was the middle of summer. Just as he was making his final point, he stopped and said, "Would someone open up a window and let some of this hot air out of here?!"

Another pastor I know opened his sermon with, "I want to welcome those of you who are perhaps here tonight."

I'm sure we've all been in similar situations at some point in our lives. Our brains mean to say one thing, but something completely different comes rolling off our tongues.

At least we don't have to worry about getting tongue-tied with God. He knows our intentions, where we're coming from. He understands us even when no one else has a clue what in the world we're talking about. He knows our words even before we speak them.

Thoughts to Ponder:

When something you say doesn't come out right, which do you think is better—clearing up the matter right away or not saying anything and hoping no one noticed it?

Tell about a time when something you said came out wrong:

Bumper Sticker for the Day:

> **God reads hearts, not just lips.**

Scripture to Stand On:

"Your Father knows what you need before you ask him."

MATTHEW 6:8

Hello Again, Lord ...

Lord, thank you for knowing what my heart is saying even when my lips are messing it up.

Twenty-seven
▲ ▼ ▲

Blanketed With Love

My mother-in-law used to live with us from time to time. Betty shared a room with my son, Matt. He had bunk beds, so she'd sleep on the bottom bunk and he'd sleep on the top.

Once, after both of them had turned in for the night, he got cold and asked if she'd get him a blanket. She did, then climbed back into her bed.

"I'm still cold, Grandma," he said. "Could you get me another blanket?"

She got him another blanket.

A short while later, he asked, "Grandma, would you mind getting me another one? I'm still cold."

If Grandma minded, she didn't say a word about it. She just got up, got him another blanket, then went back to sleep.

About ten or fifteen minutes passed, then Matt woke her up again. "Grandma, I'm hot now. Can you take one off?"

You'd think by now, Grandma would have been ready to move out and get a room at a hotel, and permanently remove his name from her will. But she didn't. She merely got up, took off one blanket, wished him good night, and went back to bed.

Now, grown and married, Matt still remembers resting there on that top bunk that night, thinking to himself, "My grandma really loves me, she really, really loves me." It's a memory of his grandmother he'll probably never forget.

Do you think that's how we must sound to God sometimes?

"Lord, I need this." Or "Lord, I need that." Or "Lord, I don't need either of those things anymore, but would you give me this one now?"

God, of course, doesn't give us everything we ask for, because some things we think we want wouldn't be good for us. He does, though, show us his love time and time again. And if we'd ever stop making requests long enough to recall how good he's already been to us, we, too, couldn't help but say, "Our God loves us. He *really, really* loves us."

Thoughts to Ponder:
List some of the ways the Lord has proven his love for you.

How does it make you feel to know that God really, really loves you?

Bumper Sticker for the Day:

There's no expiration date
on God's love.

Scripture to Stand On:
"There is only One who is good."

MATTHEW 19:17

Hello Again, Lord ...
Lord, thank you for loving me, and forgive me when I forget how very much you do.

Twenty-eight
▲▼▲

Making the Grade

A few months ago, my husband was studying for a promotion at his job. He had to read several thick books and a binder full of special material. But somehow he couldn't concentrate. He kept thinking about a problem he was having to deal with at work. He'd say to himself, *if only that problem would go away, then I could study and learn everything I need to know to pass this test.* The problem didn't go away, though, and his study time suffered. But there was nothing he could do about it.

On the day of the exam, he answered all the multiple-choice questions first. Then came the biggie—the essay question. This one question carried a lot of weight, almost half the total test points. How he answered it would be the determining factor in whether or not he passed.

So, what was the question? He couldn't believe his eyes. It was a question about the very problem that had been "interfering" with his study time. Needless to say, he had no difficulty answering the question.

We don't always recognize it, but often the turmoil we're in the middle of, that problem we desperately want to go away, contains the very lesson God wants us to learn.

Thoughts to Ponder:

Are you facing a test right now? Tell about it.

What do you think you can learn from this test?

Bumper Sticker for the Day:

> **Some of the best lessons are taught outside the classroom.**

Scripture to Stand On:

"My Father, if it is possible, may this cup be taken from me. Yet not as I will, but as you will."

MATTHEW 26:39

Hello Again, Lord ...

Lord, help me to be willing to learn all that you're wanting to teach me.

Twenty-nine

▲▼▲

What Price for a King?

It's hard to imagine one of the disciples selling out Jesus for thirty pieces of silver. But he did. That disciple, Judas Iscariot, was handpicked by our Lord to be one of the chosen twelve. Judas had celebrated the Passover with Jesus, listened to his sermons, witnessed his miracles, and was even given the trusted position of treasurer for Jesus' ministry. And yet he is the one who turned out to be our Lord's betrayer.

How could this happen, you ask? Because Judas couldn't resist the temptation of greed. His love of money, and probably his pride, became his downfall. Because Jesus wasn't assuming an earthly throne, Judas delivered him into the hands of those who would crucify him for only thirty pieces of silver. Jesus was "sold out" by a friend.

So what is it that entices us today to "sell out" Jesus? What makes us turn our backs on him? Is it popularity? "My friends won't like me if I tell them I'm a Christian."

Is it drugs? "I'll do it just this one last time, then that'll be it." It could be any number of things that tempt us away from Jesus, that get us to stop reading our Bibles, to quit going to church, to disrespect his laws. For Judas, it was thirty pieces of silver.

Sometimes we sell Jesus out for a lot less.

Thoughts to Ponder:

Is there something in your life that is causing you to "sell out" Jesus?

How do you think Jesus feels when that happens?

Bumper Sticker for the Day:

> **When you're sold out for Jesus, you won't sell him out.**

Scripture to Stand On:

Then one of the Twelve—the one called Judas Iscariot— went to the chief priests and asked, "What are you willing to give me if I hand him over to you?" So they counted out for him thirty silver coins.

MATTHEW 26:15

Hello Again, Lord ...

Lord, all the gold and silver in the world don't compare to the value of your blood shed on the cross.

Thirty
▲▼▲

Glad You're Here

I once observed an acting exercise where a participant was asked to step to the front of the room and repeat one statement over and over again until she truly believed it. The statement was simply, "I have a right to be here." Only seven words, but it was amazing to watch the range of emotions those words evoked.

At first, the statement was delivered without much feeling at all. As the actress continued to repeat the words, however, she seemed to go through a variety of feelings—intimidation, fear, pain, then determination, confidence, and self-love. It was an amazing transformation. You might want to try the exercise yourself sometime.

Each and every one of us does have a right to be here. No matter how worthless we feel at times or how insignificant others make us feel, we have a God-given right to be here. We have a right to breathe, to laugh, to cry, to eat, to walk the same earth as everyone else.

The teenage years are a vulnerable time. It's easy for someone, perhaps even a friend or a family member, to make you feel unworthy or unlovable. Thoughtless remarks, condescending attitudes, hurtful comments can cut to the bone. They can make us feel inadequate, inferior. But don't buy into those negative messages. You are valuable. You have a right to be here. And you are very, very loved. If you weren't, God wouldn't have sacrificed his own son to prove it.

Thoughts to Ponder:

Has anyone ever tried to make you feel inferior or unworthy? Tell about it.

Did that person have the power to take God's love from your life? Why not?

Bumper Sticker for the Day:

> **Looking for love in all the wrong places? Try looking to the cross.**

Scripture to Stand On:

"So don't be afraid; you are worth more than many sparrows."

MATTHEW 10:31

Hello Again, Lord ...

Lord, help me to remember the value you've placed on my life, and to treat myself accordingly.

Thirty-one
▲▼▲

Speed Limits

I'll never forget the very first traffic ticket I ever received. I was driving on the freeway, doing about 63 miles per hour (the speed limit at the time was 55). I admit it was over the speed limit, but most of the other cars were going at least 80, so I figured I was just keeping up with the flow of traffic. Unfortunately, though, in my haste I passed a police car. My heart sank when I saw its light bar flashing in my rearview mirror. I quickly and cautiously maneuvered my way to the side of the road, parked, and waited for the officer to approach.

"Clocked you at 63 miles per hour," he said, leaning into my window. "That's eight miles over the limit."

He was right, of course. I was speeding and deserved a ticket. Still, I couldn't help but ask, "But officer, didn't you see everyone else zooming past you going 80?"

He nodded, but began writing in his ticket book anyway.

"Well, if they were going 80 when they passed you, and I was only going 63 when I passed you, why'd you pick on me?"

"Because," he said, tearing off my ticket and handing it to me, "you're the only one who waved."

Have you ever passed up God like that? It's easy to do. We rush through life, going at our own speed, following our own rules, demanding our answers today, not tomorrow, this week, not next. Instead of patiently allowing him to lead, we shift into fifth gear, put the pedal to the metal, and rush on, leaving him—and his plans for our lives—behind in the dust.

Thoughts to Ponder:

Tell of a time when you may have gotten ahead of God:

Why is it important to let God take the lead position in our lives?

Bumper Sticker for the Day:

> ### Getting ahead of God will only get us behind.

Scripture to Stand On:

"Your heavenly Father knows what you need."

MATTHEW 6:32

Hello Again, Lord ...

Lord, the lead position in my life will always be reserved for you.

Thirty-two
▲▼▲

Losing to Win

It hurts to lose. It's disappointing, discouraging, and it sometimes feels like the end of the world. As strange as it sounds, though, sometimes losing can be the forerunner to an incredible blessing!

That may be hard to imagine, especially if you've just lost the cheerleading tryouts by three votes, or if your audition for the lead in that play landed you an usher job instead. But it really is true. In fact, two of my greatest opportunities came about as a result of an original rejection.

Years ago I wrote two scripts for a television show, which the producer loved. When the show was canceled, that was definitely a low moment in my life. But God brought good out of bad. The creative consultant for the canceled show also happened to be on staff with Bob Hope. He recommended me to the legendary comedian, I auditioned for him, and was soon invited to join Bob Hope's writing staff.

Another time I wrote a children's musical called "Jonah and the Whale—The Inside Story." It was rejected by a major publishing company because they had just produced one on the same topic. The editor, however, liked my work and introduced me to a young comedian friend of his, Mark Lowry. That was well over a decade ago, and I've been writing for Mark ever since.

Sure, it hurts to lose. But losing is never the end of the story, unless we allow it to be. In fact, losing can merely mean we're on the very brink of winning!

Thoughts to Ponder:

Tell about a loss that you've recently suffered:

Have you turned the matter over to the Lord? Why or why not?

Bumper Sticker for the Day:

There are no losers on God's team.

Scripture to Stand On:

"But seek first his kingdom and his righteousness, and all these things will be given to you as well."

MATTHEW 6:33

Hello Again, Lord ...

Lord, I'm always a winner when I'm with you.

Thirty-three

▲▼▲

The Blame Game

Have you ever been blamed for something you didn't do? It doesn't feel very good, does it? But don't feel bad. Sometimes people do that to God, too.

Whether it's their parents' divorce or their grandmother's death, it's all God's fault. If a computer deletes the sixty-page research paper they've been working on all night, somehow God's to blame. If they don't make the football team, it's because God didn't help them. If they get stuck in traffic, it's because God didn't open up the windows of heaven and shout, "Take an alternate route!"

Not only do they unjustly blame God for all their troubles, they punish him, too. They refuse to go to church and worship because "there are too many hypocrites there." They won't give money to support his work because they've been taken advantage of in the past by "holy manipulators." Day in and day out, they blame and punish God for things he didn't do.

But then again, false accusations are nothing new to him. Jesus was falsely accused as he stood before Pilate, and ultimately condemned to death. It was all in the plan of God, of course, but it still must have hurt as he watched his Son face all those perjured testimonies. It must hurt, too, after he's done so much good for his people, that they continually blame him for so much bad.

Thoughts to Ponder:

Is there something you're blaming God for that wasn't his fault? What is it?

Why do you think it's wrong to blame God for things that go wrong in our lives?

Bumper Sticker for the Day:

> **Why do God's children so often bite the Hand that feeds them?**

Scripture to Stand On:

"If you, then, though you are evil, know how to give good gifts to your children, how much more will your Father in heaven give good gifts to them who ask him!"

MATTHEW 7:11

Hello Again, Lord ...

Lord, thank you for being good to us 100 percent of the time.

Thirty-four

▲▼▲

Politically Correct Compassion

Years ago while picnicking at a park with a church, I watched one of the church members give some food to a homeless man who happened to walk by. It was touching. It was the Christian thing to do.

A few weeks later I watched this same lady refuse to give a soda to a young teenager visiting our church unless she forked over a buck to pay for it. The girl didn't have it.

"Sorry," the lady said. "This is a fund-raiser. We're supposed to make money, not give it away."

Now, there are teenagers (and adults) who in situations like this say they can't afford to pay simply because they are looking for a "freebie," or for some other selfish reason. This situation was different. As far as I knew, this teenager truly didn't have the dollar. More importantly, she had been going through a rough time in her life, and needed some kindness shown to her. The church lady, of course, didn't know this. She didn't bother to ask. She did, however, ask about the dollar.

"No dollar, no soda," she repeated, emphatically.

Someone did pay for the girl's soda, but the damage was done. The teenager had already been embarrassed in a room full of her peers. Technically, the church lady was right. It was a fund-raiser. But I wondered then, as I do now, what was the purpose of the fund-raising? To see how many dollar bills we could stuff into our cash box, or to see how many lives we could touch with God's love? We may have raised some money, but we missed the point.

Don't get me wrong. It was very Christlike of that woman to give food to a homeless man whom she would probably never see again. Unfortunately, we never saw that teenager in church again, either.

Thoughts to Ponder:

If you had been at the park, how would you have responded if the homeless man asked you for food? What would you have said to the thirsty girl who wanted the soda?

How do you think Jesus would have handled both situations?

Bumper Sticker for the Day:

> **Sometimes the needy look just like us.**

Scripture to Stand On:

"For I was hungry and you gave me something to eat, I was thirsty and you gave me something to drink, I was a stranger and you invited me in."

MATTHEW 25:35

Hello Again, Lord ...

Lord, help us not to be so concerned with the operations of the church that we forget its purpose.

Thirty-five

▲▼▲

Three-Ring Faith

I love the circus—parading elephants, dancing bears, daring tightrope walkers—there's nothing like it. Some circuses even feature tigers jumping through hoops of fire. (My dog jumped through a hoop of fire once while trying to escape a meatloaf explosion in my kitchen, but it wasn't the same.)

My favorite circus act is the flying trapeze. Not only are the trapeze artists incredibly brave, they have impeccable timing, too. How they can be some fifty feet above the ground and jump from one trapeze to another while executing a double or triple somersault in midair is beyond me.

Their act is so dangerous, most trapeze artists will only perform with a safety net. As dangerous as it is, though, I've never seen a trapeze artist demand *two* safety nets. I've never heard the ringmaster stop the show while a second, smaller net could be set up underneath the first, larger one. It'd look pretty silly, wouldn't it?

So why do we so often do that with God? We're in the safety of his hands, yet we still think we have to place our weak, little hands under his ... just in case. How ridiculous that must look to him. We've got the infinite span of his palm beneath us, but we still don't feel secure. We want our own safety net in place, as futile as it is. We fool ourselves into thinking that our own precautions will save us, but the simple fact is that, if we fall, his hands will be the ones to catch us, not ours.

Thoughts to Ponder:

What do you think it means to be safe in God's hands?

Talk about a time when you were glad you had that "divine safety net."

Bumper Sticker for the Day:

> **You can't slip through God's hands.
> You have to climb out.**

Scripture to Stand On:

"Are not two sparrows sold for a penny? Yet not one of them will fall to the ground apart from the will of your Father."

MATTHEW 10:29

Hello Again, Lord ...

Lord, thank you for being there when I look up and for being there to catch me whenever I look down.

Thirty-six

▲▼▲

Stop, Thief!

Have you ever been a victim of a robbery? Chances are, you'll say no. But you have. I'm sure of it. And you probably didn't even realize you were being robbed.

I'm not talking about people who steal your money or your credit cards, or who break into your house and take your entire collection of dusty soda bottles. I'm talking about people who sneak up on you when you least expect it and daringly rob you of your joy.

Joy thieves are everywhere. These mirth muggers can attack at school, at work, anywhere. They even accost their victims coming home from church, hitting them over the heads with a critical or negative comment, then snatching the blessing right out from under them. Their mission is to see how many smiles they can knock over, and how much discouragement they can spread around.

So, be on your guard. Keep your joy close to your heart and protect it at all times, because joy is a vital part of being a Christian. It's one of the best ways nonbelievers can recognize us. According to the Bible, the joy of the Lord is our very strength; it offers us protection against depression and stress.

Considering its importance, we should probably have our joy insured, but so far, no earthly insurance company has offered "joy coverage." God offers one, though, and it's found within the pages of the Bible. But unlike most insurance policies, this one requires a *daily* renewal.

Thoughts to Ponder:

Why do you think joy is important in the life of a Christian?

What kinds of things bring joy into your life?

Bumper Sticker for the Day:

> **Some of us have it backward—
> we easily surrender our smiles,
> but fight with all of our might
> to hang onto our troubles.**

Scripture to Stand On:

"Come and share your master's happiness!"

MATTHEW 25:21

Hello Again, Lord ...

Lord, help me to realize the importance of protecting your joy in my life.

Thirty-seven

▲▼▲

What's in a Name?

Did you know that God's name is holy? We hear it taken in vain so often in school, on television, in movies, and at sporting events that we can lose sight of just how holy God's name is. But God feels so strongly about us not using his name in vain that he made it one of his Ten Commandments. It's right up there with "Thou shalt not kill" and "Thou shalt not commit adultery."

God doesn't want his name used casually or angrily when our lockers won't open or when our best friend rolls over our foot with his skateboard. He doesn't want it used when our teacher assigns twenty-six pages of geometry homework, or when our VCR accidentally records the cooking channel instead of that football game we wanted to watch. When our parents tell us to take out the garbage, God doesn't expect garbage to start coming out of our mouth—especially his name being used in an irreverent way.

We're to honor God's name, revere his name, respect his name. His name should only be spoken when we're praying, praising him, telling others about him, or thanking him for his goodness. In his name there's power, unconditional love, redemption, forgiveness, and life. It's a holy name. He doesn't want us using it in unholy ways.

Thoughts to Ponder:

Why do you think God wants us to respect his name?

Have you been paying God's name the respect it deserves? Why or why not?

Bumper Sticker for the Day:

> ### God's name doesn't belong in a dictionary of slang.

Scripture to Stand On:

"This, then, is how you should pray: 'Our Father in heaven, hallowed be your name.'"

MATTHEW 6:9

Hello Again, Lord ...

Lord, help me to honor you by honoring your name.

Thirty-eight

▲▼▲

Excess Baggage

Are you still ticked off at that doctor who spanked you at birth? Or that bully on the beach who kicked sand in your face when you were eight years old? That may sound ridiculous, but some of us really do nurse ancient grudges.

I've met people in their seventies and eighties who are still bothered by something that happened fifty years ago. It's all they can talk about. It eats away at their joy and keeps them up at night. Never mind that those responsible for the hurt feelings are dead now, they still can't let the matter go.

There are times when it's not easy to let go of something that is bothering us. Just when we think we've put the matter to rest, we find ourselves taking it up again. And again. And again. It's as if by letting go, we're somehow surrendering, letting the other side win.

Actually, it's just the opposite that's true. We're winning by saying the issue isn't worth any more of our time. We have better things to do with our lives than fretting over some past injustice.

Carrying resentment, valid or not, is like carrying your winter jacket all through summer. Sure, you have every right to drag it around with you while you're surfing, skating, waterskiing, mountain biking, but why would you want to? It'll only weigh you down and wear you out. Wouldn't it be a lot better just to leave it behind and enjoy the sun?

Thoughts to Ponder:

What issue are you having a hard time letting go of?

Is this issue really worth all the energy you're giving to it?
Why or why not?

Bumper Sticker for the Day:

Life's journey
is more enjoyable
without all the carry-on baggage.

Scripture to Stand On:

"Forgive us our debts, as we also have forgiven our debtors."

MATTHEW 6:12

Hello Again, Lord ...

Lord, help me to only carry that which is good, and leave
behind the rest.

Thirty-nine
▲▼▲

Blackout

When the Northridge, California, earthquake hit in the early morning hours of January 17, 1994, every light in the city went out. I don't think there's anything more frightening than to be in utter darkness while the earth beneath you is changing zip codes. Millions of people in Southern California felt helpless, totally vulnerable. In fact, I have a feeling God heard from thousands of brand-new believers that morning.

My family and I, who live about twenty miles from the epicenter, made our way through the blackness, not knowing what dangers we would encounter on our path to safety. By some miracle, we managed to make it from the upstairs bedrooms, down the staircase, through the hallway, and out the front door without anyone getting seriously hurt.

When the sun finally began to rise, bringing its warm, reassuring light into our crisis, it was then, and only then, that we could see all the shattered glass and the maze of broken furniture through which we had walked.

Ever since God first divided the darkness from the light, light has been guiding people in the way they should go. Light casts out fear, exposes the dangers that lie ahead, and makes the journey a lot less frightening.

The light of God's love works the same way. People in darkness need his light to shine into their world and guide them to safety, too. We, as believers, have that light.

Sometimes we allow it to shine brilliantly for all to see. Sometimes we hide it under a bushel basket. And sometimes we have a full-blown blackout.

Thoughts to Ponder:

Do you know someone who could use the light of God's love in his or her life? Who?

In what ways can you show them his light?

Bumper Sticker for the Day:

> ## When ships pass in the night, are we a lighthouse ... or an iceberg?

Scripture to Stand On:

"You are the light of the world. A city on a hill cannot be hidden."

MATTHEW 5:14

Hello Again, Lord ...

Lord, help those who are searching for your light to find it in me.

Forty

▲▼▲

Never Ask Delilah
for a Trim

There's an old saying, "If a dog bites you once, it's his fault. If he bites you twice, it's *your* fault."

That's good advice. Too bad Samson didn't follow it. Samson was the strongest man on earth. The World Wrestling Federation had nothing on him. He once slew a thousand men with only the jawbone of a donkey!

Yet with all of Samson's strength, he did have one weakness. Her name was Delilah. But Delilah didn't bring down the mighty Samson on her first try. Not on her second try, either. Samson kept going back to Delilah—again and again and again, giving her the benefit of the doubt—even though it was quite obvious that she was only out to destroy him.

How could Samson have been so blind? Every time he evaded her questions by telling her a phony secret to his strength, she'd wait until he fell asleep, then use that information against him. He told her he'd lose his strength if she tied him with new ropes, so she waited until he fell asleep, then tied him with new ropes. He told her he'd lose his strength if she braided his hair, so what did she do? She waited until he fell asleep, then … wah-lah … cornrows.

Now, you'd think Samson would have gotten the hint that Delilah was up to no good. But he didn't. He kept playing along with her little game, until finally he broke down and told her the true secret to his strength—that no razor had ever touched his hair. True to form, she waited until he fell asleep again, gave him a buzz, and the rest is history.

So, was Samson's problem Delilah? Well, it may appear that way on the surface, but she really wasn't. Samson's problem was Samson. No matter how untrustworthy Delilah had proven herself to be, Samson still believed in her. The warning signs were there, but Samson refused to see them. He kept putting his trust in a dog that bites.

Thoughts to Ponder:

Why do you think Samson kept trusting Delilah when she did nothing to earn his trust?

Are there some warning signs in your life that you're refusing to read? What are they?

Bumper Sticker for the Day:

**Wisdom is knowing
when to keep your eyes open
and your mouth closed.**

Scripture to Stand On:

"Blessed are those who hunger and thirst for righteousness, for they will be filled."

MATTHEW 5:6

Hello Again, Lord ...

Lord, help me to recognize danger signals when I see them and to obey your detour signs.

Forty-one
▲▼▲

Up in the Valley

My father loved country and gospel music. He'd put the albums on the old phonograph (that was before the days of CDs) and play them over and over—Johnny Cash, Hank Williams, Patsy Cline. It was like growing up at the Grand Ol' Opry.

One record my father played quite often was "Down in the Valley." He loved that song, even though its title by no means described his attitude. My father was always "up" in the valleys of his life. He had a great outlook. No matter what came his way, he never let anything get him down.

Once, while recovering from several heart attacks, my father was scheduled to be transported from the hospital where he was staying to a nearby rehabilitation center. The driver who was to handle the transport dutifully wheeled my father up the ramp and into the medical van.

Unfortunately, the driver forgot to lock the brake on my father's wheelchair, so every time he stopped at a light, my father would roll all the way to the front of the van. Then, just as my dad started to knock on the glass divider between them, the driver would take off, sending my father rolling all the way to the back again. This went on for the entire trip! By the time they arrived at the center, my father's shirt was askew and his hair was in his face. He had every right to tell the driver off. But what did my dad do?

When the driver opened the rear doors of the van, my

father just looked at him and said, "That was better than a ride at Disneyland!" My father passed away a few months after that, but he never did lose his sense of humor.

None of us can avoid the valleys of life, but whether we're "down" in them or "up" in them is our choice.

Thoughts to Ponder:

What kind of an attitude do you have in the "valleys" of your life?

What kind of an attitude do you think God wants us to have in our "valleys"? Why?

Bumper Sticker for the Day:

> **If the joy of the Lord is our strength, would you say you're a bodybuilder or a wimp?**

Scripture to Stand On:

"Thus, by their fruit you will recognize them."

MATTHEW 7:20

Hello Again, Lord ...

Lord, help me to remember that a good attitude is the *best* testimony.

Forty-two

▲▼▲

Only You

Ever wish you could do something to change the world, but get discouraged because there's only one of you?

Well, chances are you can't change the world all by yourself, at least not all at once. But you can change it ... one act of kindness at a time.

Consider this—it only takes:

* 1 compliment to make someone feel appreciated

* 1 visit or call to end someone's loneliness

* 1 show of trust to make someone feel trustworthy

* 1 offer of hope to end someone's hopelessness

* 1 request for help to make someone feel needed

* 1 person listening to make someone feel important

* 1 burst of laughter to make others want to join in

* 1 outstretched hand to pull someone to safety

* 1 person caring to make someone feel valuable

* 1 act of forgiveness to erase someone's guilt

* 1 hug to make someone feel huggable

It only takes one person to change the world ... one act of kindness at a time.

Thoughts to Ponder:

What sorts of things do you think one person can do to help change the world for the better?

Name one person who has made a difference in your life and explain why:

Bumper Sticker for the Day:

> **How many fans does it take to get an entire stadium to start doing the wave? ... One.**

Scripture to Stand On:

"She will give birth to a son, and you are to give him the name Jesus, because he will save his people from their sins."

MATTHEW 1:21

Hello Again, Lord ...

Lord, help me not to minimize the power of one ... especially when that one is led by you.

Forty-three
▲▼▲

Down in Front!

In high school, my sister and I used to sell popcorn at football games. We'd walk through the stands with a tray of popcorn boxes strapped around our necks and yell, "Popcorn! Fifty cents! Get your popcorn here!" It was great. We could make a little money and enjoy the game at the same time.

There was only one problem. No matter how hard we tried not to, we couldn't help but block the view of the game for some very unhappy fans. "Down in front!" they'd yell. "Move it!" "Take a hike!"

I can't really say that I blame them. The crowd was there to watch the quarterback throw a winning pass or run for a sixty-yard touchdown. They weren't there to see two teenage girls selling popcorn. What we were doing was distracting them, blocking their view, and drawing their focus away from the game. So, naturally, they didn't hesitate to tell us to get out of their way.

If we're not careful, people can get in our way and block our view of Jesus, too. They move right into our line of vision, drawing our attention to them and their distracting behavior, and away from the awesome things that God is doing. We need to recognize such interferences and maintain our focus on the important matters. No matter what disturbances are going on around us, we need to say "Down in front!" and keep our eyes fixed on Jesus.

Thoughts to Ponder:

Have you allowed certain people or situations to take your eyes off the Lord?

List some ways that you can refocus your attention on more important things.

Bumper Sticker for the Day:

> **Who you see depends on who you're looking at.**

Scripture to Stand On:

"Therefore keep watch, because you do not know on what day your Lord will come."

MATTHEW 24:42

Hello Again, Lord ...

Lord, may I not let anyone or anything block my vision of you.

Forty-four
▲▼▲

No Sweat

When we're feeling unjustly persecuted or facing a problem so big we don't know what to do, we should remember three men in the Bible—Shadrach, Meshach, and Abednego (see Dn 1–3). Things got a bit heated for them, too. Shadrach, Meshach, and Abednego were thrown into a fiery furnace by King Nebuchadnezzar for refusing to bow down to a golden idol.

Now, God in his omnipotence could have easily extinguished the flames for that faithful threesome. He could have rained the fire out, blown it out, or simply spoken it out of existence. But he didn't. He didn't save the trio *from* the fire. He saved them *through* it. Shadrach, Meshach, and Abednego had to stand in the middle of the furnace and endure the trial.

But they didn't have to stand alone. God didn't say, "I'll go as far as the Prisoner's Visiting Room, and after that I'm afraid you're on your own." Nor did he say, "I *was* going to go with you, but I just overheard the guards saying they were heating the furnace to seven times hotter than usual. What'dya say I wait for you out here where there's air conditioning?"

God went with them into the furnace and stood right next to them throughout the entire ordeal, making sure not one hair on their heads was singed and not one item of clothing even picked up the smell of smoke. (You can't even walk through my kitchen without picking up the smell of smoke!)

Now, Shadrach, Meshach, and Abednego may have preferred not to go into the furnace in the first place, but that wasn't the way our Lord chose to rescue them. He chose to perform an even greater miracle, one that proved his omnipotence to the world. It also reminds us today that when we're on the "hot seat," we don't need to sweat it, either.

Thoughts to Ponder:

Why do you think God allows us to walk through a few furnaces in life?

How can we know that God will always be with us—even in the midst of our troubles?

Bumper Sticker for the Day:

> **When the heat's on, standing with God is always the coolest place to be.**

Scripture to Stand On:

"Blessed are those who are persecuted because of righteousness, for theirs is the kingdom of heaven."

MATTHEW 5:10

Hello Again, Lord ...

Lord, thank you for being a friend I can count on ... even in the "furnace."

Forty-five
▲▼▲

Sand Castles

Having grown up in Southern California, I've spent a lot of time at the beach. These days, though, I tan the easy way. I just wait for my liver spots to connect.

If you've ever been to a beach, chances are you've seen a sand castle. I've seen just about every variety imaginable—from castles that crumbled with the slightest sea breeze to elaborate forty-room medieval giants, complete with moats and drawbridges. Still, no matter how much time was spent building them, no matter how detailed and sturdy their construction, it's safe to say not one of those castles is still standing today. That's because a castle built in the sand simply can't hold up against the mighty force of the ocean waves. The laws of nature tell us that, the rules of architecture tell us that, and God's Word tells us that.

If we build our houses—or our lives—on sand, it doesn't matter how beautifully we've designed them, or how much effort we've put into them. Sooner or later they're going to fall flat. But if we build our lives on Jesus, then years later, after enduring the storms, the pounding surf, and every "El Niño" of life that comes our way, we'll still be standing.

Thoughts to Ponder:

List some ways that people build their lives upon the sand.

Name some advantages to building your life on Jesus.

Bumper Sticker for the Day:

If you want to stand, don't build on sand.

Scripture to Stand On:

"Therefore everyone who hears these words of mine, and puts them into practice is like a wise man who built his house on the rock. The rains came down, the streams rose, and the winds blew and beat against that house; yet it did not fall, because it had its foundation on the rock."

MATTHEW 7:24–25

Hello Again, Lord ...

Lord, help me to remember that it's OK to be stuck between a rock and a hard place when you're my Rock.

Forty-six
▲▼▲

Blah, Blah, Blah

Do you know someone who talks too much? Ask what's on their mind and they tell you everything, right down to their very last brain cell.

The minute you see one of these Energizer Mouths approaching, your ears probably shift into overdrive. You know a simple question such as "How are you?" is going to get a fourteen-page medical report. People like this don't believe in periods. They talk and talk and talk without ever taking a breath. Life for them is just one long run-on sentence, and absolutely nothing stops them from getting in the last word. Even their tombstone will probably say, "And another thing …"

Compulsive talkers seem to fear there'll be a lull in the conversation if they dare to take a break, if they dare breathe. The truth is, though, if they'd just be quiet and let someone else talk for awhile, they might end up actually *having* a conversation. They might even learn something, too. We learn a lot more when we're listening than when we're talking. Maybe that's why God gave us two ears, two eyes … and only one mouth!

Thoughts to Ponder:

What kinds of things do you think a person who talks too much misses by not listening more?

Have there been times when you wished you had listened more and talked less? Tell about it.

Bumper Sticker for the Day:

> **When we give an account for each word we've spoken, it's going to take some people an eternity.**

Scripture to Stand On:

"For by your words you will be acquitted, and by your words you will be condemned."

MATTHEW 12:37

Hello Again, Lord ...

Lord, help me to remember that the sound of my own voice shouldn't be the only sound I hear.

Forty-seven
▲ ▼ ▲

High-Fashion Pork

When I was a teenager, I spent some time on my uncle's farm. I rode on the tractor as he drove around the fields picking up freshly baled hay. I watched him milk cows, gather eggs from the chicken coop, and even feed the pigs.

Being a city girl, I'd never seen a pigpen before, so I found that especially interesting. All those pigs had to do all day was eat and sleep. They even got to sleep in their food! (It was sort of like having a slumber party inside an all-you-can-eat salad bar!)

Those pigs had it made. They didn't have to worry about homework, finals, or making the basketball team. They didn't even have to worry about what they were going to wear the next day. You'll never see a pig in Levi's and a tank top (OK, maybe in California). You'll never catch one wearing a string of pearls, either. The Bible even tells us that. (You didn't know the Good Book gave animal fashion tips, did you?)

In Matthew 7:6, Jesus warns us about casting our pearls before swine. He knew that pigs can't appreciate pearls. Can't eat 'em, can't wear 'em. The porkers just trample those glistening gems underfoot and continue partying in the mud.

What do you suppose Jesus meant when he gave this fine jewelry tip? After all, who would be foolish enough to waste something as valuable as a pearl on mere pigs? And yet, have you ever tried to share your "pearls"—those things that are most important to you—with someone who just didn't appreciate what you had to offer? Jesus wants you to know that your pearls haven't lost any of their worth. You just need to brush off the dust, put them carefully in your pocket, and ask the Lord for wisdom. He will let you know when the time is right to bring them out again!

Thoughts to Ponder:
What kind of "pearls" do you think Jesus was referring to?

Do you have any "pigs" stepping on the "pearls" in your life? How are you handling the situation?

Bumper Sticker for the Day:

> ## A pearl is still a pearl, no matter how much mud gets kicked on it.

Scripture to Stand On:
"Do not give dogs what is sacred; do not throw your pearls to pigs. If you do, they may trample them under their feet, and then turn and tear you to pieces."

MATTHEW 7:6

Hello Again, Lord ...
Lord, help me to cherish and protect the "pearls" that you have entrusted to me.

Forty-eight
▲▼▲

One Thousand Three Hundred and Counting ...

Ever get tired of forgiving the people in your life who keep hurting you? They hurt you, you forgive. They hurt you again, you forgive them again. They hurt you a third, fourth, fifth, and sixth time. You forgive a third, fourth, fifth, and sixth time. It's like a bad movie that keeps running over and over, and you wish that you could rewrite the script—or at least play a different role. You're tired of always being the forgiving one.

In Matthew 18:21-22, Peter came to Jesus and asked, "Lord, how many times shall I forgive my brother when he sins against me? Up to seven times?" "No!" Jesus replied. "Seventy times seven!" (TLB).

All right—get out a calculator. Seventy times seven is ... ummm ... Wow! That's a lot of forgiveness. Certainly more than this person deserves. But that's what Jesus told us we're to do.

Now, don't get confused. That doesn't mean we're supposed to be a doormat and let someone continually walk all over us. It just means we're to keep the door to our heart open when we're asked to forgive. Not once. Not twice. Not even seventy times!

Seventy times seven. That sounds like a lot. Then again, aren't you glad God doesn't put a cap on how many times he extends his forgiveness to us?

Thoughts to Ponder:

What do you think makes some people continually hurt others?

Is there something for which you need to forgive someone today?

Bumper Sticker for the Day:

**Forgiveness—
the gift that keeps on giving.**

Scripture to Stand On:

"Blessed are the merciful, for they will be shown mercy."

MATTHEW 5:7

Hello Again, Lord ...

Lord, help me to forgive as often as you forgive me.

Forty-nine

▲▼▲

Copycat

Imagine what it would be like to copy off someone else's test ... then fail anyway because that person hadn't studied, either. Pretty embarrassing, huh? That's just one good reason why cheating is a bad idea. The number one reason, of course, is it's against the Bible. (Remember? "Thou shalt not covet anything that is thy neighbor's." That includes his answer sheet.)

The best way to ensure a passing grade on any test, and maybe even gain some knowledge in the process, is to study for yourself. That's the best way to pass life's tests, too. Don't blindly copy the solution God may have given someone else for their need. He could have a completely different one for your situation—equally as good, but tailored specifically for you.

Throughout the Bible, God used a variety of rescues for his children. He parted the Red Sea for Moses, closed the lions' mouths for Daniel, cooled the fire for Shadrach, Meshach, and Abednego, and brought down the mighty wall of Jericho for Joshua. He's pretty creative.

Now, had Daniel asked God to part the Red Sea, like he had done for Moses, it wouldn't have done Daniel much good. Daniel didn't need to cross the Red Sea. He was in the den with a bunch of hungry lions. He needed a different kind of deliverance.

Had Shadrach prayed for the walls of the furnace to fall

down like they had done for Joshua, there might not have been any walls left, but the three men still would have had to contend with the fire.

God knew precisely how best to deliver each of these people. He knows precisely what you need in your situation, too. God's answers are always good, always perfect, always worth waiting for … and they'll always be custom-made for you.

Thoughts to Ponder:
Name some other people in the Bible whose prayers God answered in a unique way.

Have you had a situation in your life for which God gave you a custom answer? Tell about it:

Bumper Sticker for the Day:

> **The best way to pass life's tests is to study God's textbook yourself.**

Scripture to Stand On:
Jesus replied, "You are in error because you do not know the Scriptures or the power of God."

MATTHEW 22:29

Hello Again, Lord …
Lord, help me to remember that when I'm in the middle of my problems, you're in the middle of my answers.

Fifty
▲ ▼ ▲

Joy Journaling

It's good to keep a daily journal. But don't just record your struggles, your broken heart, and your hurt feelings. Write down the good things, too. In fact, why not start a "Joy Journal"?

A Joy Journal is like a regular journal, except absolutely no negative comments or thoughts are allowed in it. It's a place to write down those things in your life that make you happy, bring a smile to your face, or make you feel loved. A Joy Journal is a register of the positive things you've experienced. It's an accounting of your blessings. Whenever you're feeling down, you can open your Joy Journal and get that emotional lift you need.

We all have positive things that happen to us, overwhelmingly more than negative. But for some reason, the negative stands out in our memories so much more. Keeping an account of those good times helps us all cope a little better when the bad times come.

Life here on earth is going to be full of ups and downs. Discouragement and disappointment are a normal part of our earthly experience. But if we focus on these times too much we will look back on the book of our lives and discover there are whole chapters missing. The *best* chapters.

Thoughts to Ponder:

Write down something good that's happened in your life that you never want to forget:

If you do keep a journal, would you say that most of your entries are positive or negative?

Bumper Sticker for the Day:

> **Journaling your blessings
> is like sending
> a thank-you note to God.**

Scripture to Stand On:

"Do you still not understand? Don't you remember the five loaves for the five thousand, and how many basketfuls you gathered?"

MATTHEW 16:9

Hello Again, Lord ...

Lord, help me to remember that blessings are like new telephone numbers. If we don't write them down, we tend to forget them.

Fifty-one

▲▼▲

He's With Me

Some teenagers like to pretend they have no parents. They make Mom or Dad drop them off at least three blocks away from school so no one will see them getting out of the family car. They insist their parents use an alias on Back-to-School Night, wear a disguise whenever they chaperone youth group outings, and maintain at least a twenty-foot distance behind them at the mall. If Mom gets that "Can I have a hug?" look in her eye, they break out into a cold sweat and have the entire area swept for hidden cameras.

I'm sure *you* don't do any of these things, so I won't even talk about that kind of misplaced embarrassment. Today's devotional is about something even more serious. It's about being embarrassed by your faith.

Are you ashamed of God? Do you make him stay at least three blocks away from your school, too, or do you invite him to come onto the campus with you? Do you mumble when you introduce him to your friends, like you do with your Uncle Milton (who talks to the shrubbery)? Or is your relationship with Jesus so important to you that you are proud to say his name?

Being ashamed of your parents isn't right. Being ashamed of your Uncle Milton might be understandable ... but it isn't right, either. Your faith is something you should never be ashamed of, though. As Christians, we shouldn't hesitate to stand up for Jesus with the same courage that he showed when he stood up for us as he hung on the cross.

Thoughts to Ponder:
Have you ever felt embarrassed about your faith? Tell about it:

How do you think that made Jesus feel?

Bumper Sticker for the Day:

God's army doesn't need
undercover agents.

Scripture to Stand On:
"Whoever acknowledges me before men, I will also acknowledge him before my Father in heaven."

MATTHEW 10:32

Hello Again, Lord ...
Lord, thank you for never being ashamed of me. May I always treat you likewise.

Fifty-two
▲▼▲

Me, Me, Me, Me, Me

Singing "me, me, me, me, me" is a great way to warm up your vocal chords. *Thinking* "me, me, me, me, me" is a great way to lose all your friends.

Do you know someone who thinks only of himself, whose entire focus is inward? Some people are like that. It's as if no one else exists on this planet. They hog the road when they drive and the conversation when they talk. Their sole concern in any situation is how circumstances will affect their own happiness. Everything is me, me, me.

In his Word, God has a lot to say about people like that. He says, "For men to search their own glory is not glory," and that "pride goeth before destruction, and a haughty spirit before a fall" (Prv 16:18).

The Bible says a lot about humility, too. It says that God honors and gives grace to the lowly, that he promises to save the humble person, and that he will not forget their cries. In other words, according to God, the back of the line is the best place to be.

Thoughts to Ponder:

Why do some people think only of themselves?

Why do you think God honors the humble?

Bumper Sticker for the Day:

He who holds his own spotlight usually ends up getting burned.

Scripture to Stand On:

"And whoever wants to be first must be your slave."

MATTHEW 20:27

Hello Again, Lord ...

Lord, help me to remember that my promotions always come from you.

Fifty-three

▲ ▼ ▲

Going Under

When I was a teenager I almost drowned on a youth retreat with my church. Drowning wasn't on the list of approved activities, but it wasn't my fault.... Well, on second thought, maybe it was.

You see, I was joking around with our youth pastor. We were in the swimming pool and every time he'd go under the water, I'd swim over to where he was and stand on his back. He played along for awhile, until he decided he needed to breathe (go figure) and knocked me off.

Our little game was fun as long as we were in the shallow end. But when he swam to the deep end, with me on his back, standing on him quickly became a necessity. I couldn't swim.

When he knocked me off this time, I went down ... and down ... and down. Under the water, I could hear the rest of the youth group laughing and having a great time. I was only a few feet away from them, yet not one person noticed I was drowning.

After swallowing most of the recommended daily intake of eight glasses of water, I finally heard someone yell, "Hey, I think she's drowning!" Within seconds the youth pastor pulled me to safety.

Thankfully for me, the story has a happy ending. But I wonder how many people are within earshot of our laughter and conversation, people we see day in and day out, who are drowning in a pool of loneliness and despair, heartache and pain, and no one's noticing.

Thoughts to Ponder:

Why do you think it's important to pay attention to those around us?

Have you ever felt like you were drowning and no one noticed?

Bumper Sticker for the Day:

> **The best life preserver is God's love.
> Rescue someone with it today.**

Scripture to Stand On:

"Because of the increase of wickedness, the love of most will grow cold."

MATTHEW 24:12

Hello Again, Lord ...

Lord, open my eyes that I might see the pain of those who cross my path today.

Fifty-four
▲▼▲

If I Had Your Life to Live Over Again

Have you ever listened to a sermon and thought to yourself, *This is the perfect message for so-and-so.* "Darla should have been here. This is *exactly* what she needs to hear!" Or "Boy, could Kevin have used this sermon! I knew I should have insisted that he come with me to church today!"

But did you ever stop to think that the ones God most wants to hear the sermon are already in church? Is it possible that he inspired the pastor to preach that sermon just for *you?* (Gulp.)

Christians aren't perfect. We're not even close. When judged by God's standards, we *all* fall short. Even so, we spend much of our time fretting over the imperfections of other people. It's so much easier to see what others are doing wrong with their lives than to recognize how *we're* messing up.

The Bible warns us of this kind of behavior. It says it's like having a plank in our own eye while trying to remove the splinter from our brother's eye. Instead of having 20-20 vision, we've got "2x4 vision." In other words, if we spent as much time and effort improving ourselves as we spend trying to improve others, we'd all be a lot better off.

Thoughts to Ponder:

Which do you spend more time on: trying to change others or trying to change yourself?

Why do you think God wants us to regularly examine our own lives?

Bumper Sticker for the Day:

Change within ourselves can start a chain reaction of change in others.

Scripture to Stand On:

"You hypocrite, first take the plank out of your own eye, and then you will see clearly to remove the speck from your brother's eye."

MATTHEW 7:5

Hello Again, Lord ...

Lord, if my spiritual vision needs correcting, help me to follow your prescription.

Fifty-five
▲▼▲

Whys Guy?

Have you ever asked God "Why?"

"Why didn't I make the football team?"

"Why didn't I win a spot on the cheerleading squad?"

"Why didn't that cute guy in algebra class answer that note I discreetly taped to the back of his head?"

Then, there are those big questions in life. The questions adults have a difficult time answering:

"Why did my parents have to divorce?"

"Why did my grandfather have to die?"

"Why is my best friend's mom suffering from cancer?"

Adults may have a difficult time answering our tough questions, but God doesn't. He'll answer each and every one of them. If not here and now, then in eternity.

I've asked God a lot of "whys" in my life. I married when I was just eighteen, and by the time I was twenty I'd had a three-month miscarriage and a nine-month stillbirth. That really hurt. But God is faithful. My husband and I later adopted two sons—and became the biological parents of a third son—all within two years!

No matter why we are hurting, we can trust God to help us through our grief. When the sparrow falls, he knows about it and he cares. Our tears are no different. He knows when each one of them falls. He loved us enough to give his life for us. He loves us enough to handle our "whys".

Thoughts to Ponder:

What "why" question would you like to ask God?

Why do you think it's important to trust God even when things don't make sense?

Bumper Sticker for the Day:

> **If we're "leaning on the everlasting arms," we don't have to worry about slipping through them.**

Scripture to Stand On:

But Jesus immediately said to them: "Take courage! It is I. Don't be afraid."

MATTHEW 14:27

Hello Again, Lord ...

Lord, when I don't understand, help me to lean on your understanding.

Fifty-six
▲ ▼ ▲

Will the Real "You" Please Stand Up?

Some years ago, an organization to which I belong invited a famous science fiction writer, Ray Bradbury, as a special guest speaker. Mr. Bradbury doesn't drive, so the president of the group asked my husband and me if we'd mind picking him up. We were thrilled to do it, but I did have one slight reservation.

"We can't pick him up in *our car*," I said to my husband.

"What's wrong with our car?" he asked.

"You mean besides the fact that it stalls out on speed bumps, and the front passenger window won't roll up?"

My husband didn't see my point. He was sure Mr. Bradbury wouldn't mind. He thought that the car might even give him ideas for his next science fiction novel.

Thankfully, some friends of ours came to my rescue and offered to let us borrow their Cadillac for the evening. It was perfect. We'd be able to pick up Mr. Bradbury in style, and our old car wouldn't embarrass us. Things were really working out, I figured. But ...

Have you ever heard the saying, "The best-laid plans of mice and men often go astray"? As soon as Ray Bradbury was in the borrowed Cadillac, it began to rain. Not just sprinkle. *Rain!*

My husband tried to find the button that controlled the windshield wipers, but opened the sunroof instead. Then, in an effort to locate the defrost button, he mistakenly turned on the air conditioner and disengaged the lock on the trunk. Needless to say, the trip was quite an adventure.

Some good did come out of the evening, though. We learned it's always better, drier, and a whole lot less embarrassing just to be yourself!

Thoughts to Ponder:

Have you ever tried to be something you aren't? Tell about it.

Why do you think it's always better to be yourself?

Bumper Sticker for the Day:

> **If you're busy being someone else, who's being you?**

Scripture to Stand On:

"For whoever exalts himself will be humbled."

MATTHEW 23:12

Hello Again, Lord ...

Lord, help me to remember that the "real" me is always the "best" me.

Fifty-seven
▲▼▲

Knock, Knock

For the first five years of my marriage, I sold cosmetics door-to-door. During that time, I learned some very basic facts of life. I learned a Chihuahua's jaw span is precisely the size of my ankle. (Every time I visited this one customer, her Chihuahua would attach itself to me like some sort of canine ankle bracelet, and no matter how hard I tried to shake him loose, he wouldn't let go. I was his own personal human chewstick.)

I also learned that strawberry lipstick samples left too long in a hot car will turn into strawberry soup. (It doesn't taste so bad, but it sure leaves a stain around your mouth.)

And I learned that if you want people to open their door to you, you've got to *knock*.

The Bible tells us that if we want something from the Lord, we need to knock, too. We need to verbalize our requests. He already knows our needs even before we ask, but he still wants to hear us say the words. Why? Because asking demonstrates faith.

If Bill Gates, one of the richest men in the world, was our father, would we hesitate to ask him for the things we needed? Of course not. Then why do we hesitate to ask the One who created Bill Gates, the One who made the universe and everything else in it, for the things we need?

Thoughts to Ponder:

Are you in need of something for which you haven't yet asked God?

What do you think is keeping you from asking him?

Bumper Sticker for the Day:

Knock, knock.
Who's there?
God—yesterday, today, and forever.

Scripture to Stand On:

"For everyone who asks receives; he who seeks finds; and to him who knocks, the door will be opened."

MATTHEW 7:8

Hello Again, Lord ...

Lord, thank you for being there whenever I knock.

Fifty-eight

▲▼▲

Where There's Smoke,
There's Turkey

A few years ago Mark Lowry sent me a smoked turkey for Christmas. It was, according to his enthusiastic endorsement, some of the best turkey in the world. Unfortunately, I didn't get to test that claim because I didn't take time to read the directions. Not knowing the word "smoked" meant "fully cooked," I assumed I should roast the bird the same way I do all my turkeys: in a 350-degree oven until tender, or until the firemen arrive, whichever comes first.

For the entire time that turkey was roasting, everything seemed to be going fine. There weren't any dark clouds billowing out of the oven. There was no odor of burning meat. My smoke alarm didn't even go off.

But when I finally took that poor bird out of the oven, some fourteen hours later, and pulled back the aluminum foil covering it, I couldn't believe my eyes. The poor thing looked as if it'd been struck by lightning! Twice! It was as black as a pair of army boots, and about as tender. Its poor legs were pointing in opposite directions, and the meat on each drumstick had shrunk, leaving four inches of bare bone protruding in the air. Had the SPCA seen it, I'd still be paying off the fine!

Just like that turkey, life comes with its own set of directions. They're found in God's Word, the Holy Bible. But too often we don't take the time to read what it says, and we get burned. We then stand back, assess the mess we're in, and ask what in the world went wrong. The answer is simple: we forgot to read the directions.

Thoughts to Ponder:

Is there a time when you didn't follow God's directions?

What would you do differently if you had the chance?

Bumper Sticker for the Day:

God's Word— our Thomas Guide for life.

Scripture to Stand On:

"For whoever does the will of my Father in heaven is my brother and sister and mother."

MATTHEW 12:50

Hello Again, Lord ...

Lord, when I don't know which way I should go, I'm glad *you* do.

Fifty-nine

▲▼▲

Hide-and-Seek

When I was young, one of my favorite games was "hide-and-seek." I'd pick great places to hide—in the kitchen cupboard, between the sofa cushions, under my bed. Sometimes it'd be hours before anyone found me. Sometimes it'd be hours before anyone *looked* for me.

Did you know it's good to get alone with God like that? Not necessarily in the kitchen cupboard (you might scare your little brother while he's looking for his cereal), but it's good to "hide away" in some quiet place and seek God. It may be in your backyard, a park, or just alone in a bedroom. The location doesn't really matter.

Life can get hectic at times. Between church, school, sports, music lessons, friends, and family, it can be tough to find a quiet moment. When the television's blaring, the phone's ringing, the stereo's blasting, and the dog's barking (why he can't just eat my leftovers and be quiet about it is beyond me), it's hard to hear God.

So, why not take a moment today to "hide" and "seek" him? And if you're quiet, really quiet, you just might be surprised at how much you hear.

Thoughts to Ponder:

Why do you think it's important to get alone with God?

Where is a good place for you to get alone with God?

131

Bumper Sticker for the Day:

**When God calls,
don't put him on hold.**

Scripture to Stand On:

"But when you pray, go into your room, close the door and pray to your Father, who is unseen. Then your Father, who sees what is done in secret, will reward you."

MATTHEW 6:6

Hello Again, Lord ...

Lord, remind me that it's in the quiet moments that the most important things can be heard.

Sixty

▲▼▲

It's in the Genes

We probably all know someone who blames their bad behavior on circumstances beyond their control.

"I was born this way."

"My parents act like this so I have to act like this, too."

"It's too late for me to change."

"I had sugar overload. That's why I was hang gliding from the roof of the school cafeteria."

It's easy to come up with excuses for our bad temper, selfishness, and lack of self-control. On the other hand, accepting responsibility for our own actions is the first step toward true maturity.

When something makes us angry, we can choose to control our tongues and our tempers, or we can let the expletives fly. It's up to us.

When we're given an opportunity to put our own needs on hold so that someone else's need can be met, the choice is ours. We can make the sacrifice or tell them to lump it.

Ultimately, we will all have to answer to God for our own actions. No one else is responsible for the things we do... not our parents, our friends, or even the doctor who brought us into the world. Just us. So the next time we face circumstances that test our self-control, we can give in to the temptation or we can determine to be in control. The decision is ours.

Thoughts to Ponder:

Are there some areas in your life for which you're constantly making excuses?

What are some ways to start changing those behaviors today?

Bumper Sticker for the Day:

> **Are you making changes
> or just excuses?**

Scripture to Stand On:

Another disciple said to him, "Lord, first let me go and bury my father."

MATTHEW 8:21

Hello Again, Lord ...

Lord, if I'm going to follow anyone else's behavior, let it be yours.

Sixty-one

▲▼▲

All Work and No Play

Are you a compulsive overachiever? Do you spend all your free time at the library realphabetizing the books? Are you so exhausted that you find yourself using your mashed potatoes as a pillow at the dinner table? Are you getting so little sleep that you're having to fast-forward your dreams?

There are twenty-four hours in the day. God didn't intend for us to work twenty-three of them. He expects us to use wisdom when it comes to our daily schedules. If we're working and studying every minute of every day, we probably should be asking ourselves why. If it's to prove something to someone else or gain approval, then we're simply spinning our wheels. That's not how to gain approval. It's how to gain a hospital bed.

Perhaps we're pushing ourselves for other reasons. We might be pushing ourselves so we'll have enough money to buy everything we've ever wanted. If so, it might be time to adjust some of our priorities. Maybe we can do without that snowboard, or that new outfit, or those $100 shoes. What we truly might be needing instead is a good night's sleep, and that doesn't cost a single dime.

Don't misunderstand me. There's nothing wrong with good, hard work and achieving the goals we set out to accomplish. It's admirable. But there needs to be balance. Success shouldn't come at the price of our health. Besides, if we're doing all the working, all the planning, and opening all the career doors ourselves, what are we leaving in God's hands?

Thoughts to Ponder:

Why does God want us to "rest" in him?

What do you think makes some people push themselves to the breaking point?

Bumper Sticker for the Day:

> **If God didn't think rest was important, he would have worked overtime on the seventh day.**

Scripture to Stand On:

"Come to me, all you who are weary and burdened, and I will give you rest."

MATTHEW 11:28

Hello Again, Lord ...

Lord, whenever I'm driving myself too hard, help me to remember that life shouldn't be all work and no play. It should be some work, some play, and a whole lot of pray.

Sixty-two
▲▼▲

Food for Thought

The Bible tells us that our bodies are temples of the Holy Spirit, so it's important that we pay attention to what we're putting into them. I learned this the hard way.

Being diabetic, I try to keep some sort of candy in my purse at all times, just in case my blood sugar level starts to plummet. One Sunday morning, however, there wasn't any candy in the house, so I grabbed a box of raisins that I had bought on sale at a local store, tucked it into my purse, then headed off to church.

About midway through the sermon, I started feeling the symptoms of a low blood sugar reaction. Not wanting to disturb those seated around me by getting up and leaving the sanctuary, I remained in my seat, maintained eye contact with the pastor, and began discreetly lifting a handful of raisins to my mouth at regular intervals.

As I was doing this, I glanced down and happened to notice a little white wormlike creature making its way across my blouse. I knocked it off and looked around the pew to see where it might have come from. Seeing nothing out of the ordinary, I resumed eating the raisins, my eyes still fixed on the pastor.

A few minutes later, another white wormlike creature started making its way across my leg. I knocked him off, too. *Where are they coming from?* I thought to myself.

Suddenly, I got a sinking feeling. I turned the box of

raisins over and opened the opposite end. There they were—ten or twenty of them, eating raisins at that end as fast as I was eating them from the other.

I learned a good lesson that day about eating in church, about buying outdated raisins, and most importantly, about paying attention to the things I put in my mouth.

Thoughts to Ponder:
Why do you think God instructs us to take care of our bodies?

Is there something you're putting into your body that you shouldn't?

Bumper Sticker for the Day:

> **Take good care of your body.
> You represent its Maker.**

Scripture to Stand On:
"Give us today our daily bread."

MATTHEW 6:11

Hello Again, Lord ...
Lord, thank you for choosing our bodies to be the dwelling place of the Holy Spirit. May he always feel welcome and appreciated.

Sixty-three
▲ ▼ ▲

Doors

Each year we pass through a lot of doors—front doors, back doors, revolving doors, automatic doors, sliding glass doors, car doors, classroom doors, airplane doors, doggie doors (OK, so I've locked myself out of the house a few times). But this chapter isn't about those kinds of doors. It's about the doors that God opens and closes for us throughout our lives.

Have you ever prayed for God to open a certain door—only to see another, seemingly insignificant door open instead? I've found that often it's those doors, those "hallway" doors of life, that are the very ones that lead to the best opportunities. They may not look very promising on the outside, but they could be the only path to the door God really wants you to walk through.

God has promised to lead and guide us. But sometimes he wants to see if we're going to be obedient. He wants to know that we're willing to follow him even when we don't exactly know where he's leading. He may be testing us to see if we'll humble ourselves enough to walk through that hallway door to his blessings, or if we're just going to stand on the outside and complain.

Thoughts to Ponder:

Have you ever prayed for God to open one door for you, and found that he opened another one instead? What did you do?

Why do you think God wants us to trust him to open the right doors in our lives, and to close the wrong ones?

Bumper Sticker for the Day:

When God closes a door, it's not a good idea to dynamite your way through it anyway.

Scripture to Stand On:

As Jesus went on from there, he saw a man named Matthew sitting at the tax collector's booth. "Follow me," he told him, and Matthew got up and followed him.

MATTHEW 9:9

Hello Again, Lord ...

Lord, may I never hesitate to walk through the doors you open and away from the ones you close.

Sixty-four
▲▼▲

For He's a Jolly Good Target

Have you ever watched a gossip in action? Their tongue moves so fast, you wonder how it keeps from getting whiplash. You also wonder why it needs to move that fast, when chances are, it's only telling half the story.

Gossips thrive on telling half-stories. And believe it or not, some people thrive on hearing them. Half-truths can easily take on a life of their own. I was recently reminded of this by an experience in my own life.

I'm president of a writing group in the town where I live. At one of our meetings, I passed out a lot of material to the attendees—paper after paper after paper. After the meeting, our newsletter editor jokingly reported in our monthly mailer that my family and I had purchased a paper factory, and that's how I could distribute so many handouts. Those who were at the meeting all got the joke, but then I started receiving congratulatory messages from people who weren't at the meeting. Our state board picked up the news and ran it in their California state newsletter. A local newspaper columnist even called and wanted to do a feature story on me and my new paper factory!

We all had a good laugh over it. And yet, that's how gossip works. Half-stories quickly become truth to those who don't bother to find out the other side of the story. To this day, there are probably those who still think I own a paper factory. Luckily, that was innocent false information.

No one was hurt because of it. But can you see how damaging incorrect information about someone's reputation can be?

The Ten Commandments tell us not to bear false witness. In other words, it's a sin. So the next time you hear something negative about someone, especially a friend, go to that person and give him or her a chance to verify the story. That's not gossip. That's getting the facts straight. To do anything less, you can't truly call yourself a friend. To do anything less isn't very Christian, either.

Thoughts to Ponder:

Have you ever repeated something about someone you heard without checking out the facts first?

Do you think that was fair? Why or why not?

Bumper Sticker for the Day:

**When you hear gossip,
be a skeptic ... not a sponge.**

Scripture to Stand On:

"But I tell you that men will have to give account on the day of judgment for every careless word they have spoken."

MATTHEW 12:36

Hello Again, Lord ...

Lord, help me to keep the doors of my lips closed, and sometimes, Lord, help me to deadbolt them.

Sixty-five
▲▼▲

Too Smart for Their
Own Eternal Good

Have you ever gotten into a debate with someone over whether or not there is a God? They challenge you to prove God's existence, then turn a deaf ear to anything you have to say. They refuse to read the Bible with an objective mind or listen to any facts you present. Their opinion is already etched in stone.

The sad thing about people like this is they're too smart for their own eternal good. They think their doubts can keep God from existing, but it doesn't work that way. God does exist, always has and always will, in spite of their skepticism, in spite of their unbelief. Contrary to what they think, God's not afraid to answer their questions. They just have to look in the right place—in the Word of God—with an open heart and mind.

We're all going to stand before the Creator one day. It's not going to matter then how well any of us could debate our position on his existence. It's not going to matter whose car had the Christian fish, whose car had the Darwin fish, or whose car had the Christian fish eating the Darwin fish. The only thing that's going to matter then is whether or not our names are written in the Lamb's Book of Life. And that requires faith. Faith, and a whole lot of sense!

Thoughts to Ponder:

Do you know someone who doubts God's existence?

What can you do to help open his or her eyes to the truth?

Bumper Sticker for the Day:

> ### Does God exist?
> ### Why don't you ask him?

Scripture to Stand On:

"What good will it be for a man if he gains the whole world, yet forfeits his soul?"

MATTHEW 16:26

Hello Again, Lord ...

Lord, open the eyes of those who doubt you, that they may *know* you.

Sixty-six

▲▼▲

The Perfect Answer

Jesus came face to face with legalism—that attitude that makes people overlook grace and pay more attention to the law than they do to the One who made the law. In Matthew 12, the Pharisees tried to trap Jesus (again) by pointing out a man with a withered hand, then asking Jesus if it would be lawful for him to heal the man on the Sabbath day.

Their first mistake was assuming that it was *work* for Jesus to heal the man. All Jesus had to do was speak the word and the man would be made whole. There wasn't any work involved. Plenty of power, but no work.

The Pharisees thought they had Jesus. They knew the "law" and assumed Jesus would have no politically correct way to answer their question. But Jesus turned the tables on them, answering their questions with one of his own. He asked if one of their sheep were to fall into a pit on the Sabbath, would they lift it out of the hole?

The Pharisees thought for a moment, but didn't have a comeback. They just stood there, embarrassed and speechless, while Jesus proceeded to heal the man.

Jesus was good at turning the tables on legalism. Whenever self-righteous people thought they had him trapped, Jesus would usually bring the matter around to love. And when it's a judgment call between the two, with Jesus, love always wins out.

Thoughts to Ponder:

Do you know of a situation where love won out over legalism? Tell about it.

What do you think of when you hear the words "God's grace"?

Bumper Sticker for the Day:

> ### The problem with legalism is it's so seldom self-imposed.

Scripture to Stand On:

"Do not think that I have come to abolish the Law or the Prophets; I have not come to abolish them but to fulfill them."

MATTHEW 5:17

Hello Again, Lord ...

Lord, remind me that your greatest commandments are to love you with all my heart, soul, and mind, and to love my neighbor as myself.

Sixty-seven

▲▼▲

Lights, Camera, Action!

When the director of a film or television show wants the actors to begin performing, he usually says, "Action!" It's an important word. At that moment, only one thing matters: the actor's performance. Nothing else. Not the actor's reputation, not his agent's promises. Just what is happening on stage right then.

It's like that in life, too. Do you know that what we do is far more important than what we say we're going to do? If your friend tells you he'll be happy to pick you up after volleyball practice, but doesn't show up, do you remember his willingness to volunteer or his failure to follow through? Chances are, as you're walking home in the rain with no jacket, you're going to remember his failure to follow through.

Following through on our promises is especially important when it comes to the Lord's work. We can have a "To Do" list a mile long, written with all the best intentions, but if nothing ever gets checked off it, we're no better than the person who never volunteers for anything.

"We need someone to clean out the Choir Room."

"I'm there!"

"We could sure use some help with the church newsletter."

"You can count on me!"

"We need a volunteer to plan the games for the Valentine's Banquet."

"Sign me up!"

It's great when people volunteer, but that's the easy part. God doesn't need workers who talk a good game, but never accomplish anything. He doesn't want hands that just volunteer. He wants hands that'll also get the job done.

Thoughts to Ponder:

Is there a job for which you've volunteered, but haven't yet followed through?

What steps can you take today toward completing that task?

Bumper Sticker for the Day:

God needs our muscles,
not just our mouths.

Scripture to Stand On:

"What do you think? There was a man who had two sons. He went to the first and said, 'Son, go and work today in the vineyard.' 'I will not,' he answered, but later he changed his mind and went. Then the father went to the other son and said the same thing. He answered, 'I will, sir,' but he did not go. Which of the two did what his father wanted?" "The first," they answered.

MATTHEW 21:28-31

Hello Again, Lord ...

Lord, remind me to always start what I promise, and finish what I start.

Sixty-eight

▲▼▲

Now I Lay Me Down to Sleep

Do you know someone who can fall asleep anywhere—at school, at church, in a dental chair during a root canal? Personally, I have a hard time sleeping when I'm not in my own bed. I'm used to my own pillow, my own blankets, and my own lumps ... in the mattress, that is, not my body. (Although I'm pretty used to those lumps, too.)

I wasn't always such a picky sleeper. When I was young, I had no trouble falling asleep in uncomfortable places—like the family car. Often, my father would drive us to gospel quartet concerts in cities that were at least an hour's drive away. The hum of the engine and the gentle motion of the car would get me dozing faster than a monotone reading of the genealogies. I'd be so deep in sleep, I wouldn't wake up until the next morning, when I'd mysteriously find myself safe and sound in my own bed.

It didn't take much investigation to find out how I had gotten there. It was my father who, figuring it'd be easier than trying to wake me up, would carry me into the house and tuck me into bed.

Now, as an adult, I don't sleep in cars anymore. First of all, I'm a lot bigger now and I don't think anyone would carry me into the house. And second, these days I'm usually the one driving, so I can't fall asleep. Well, I *could*, but the Highway Patrol frowns on drivers who purposely release their airbags to use as pillows.

Still, I'll never forget the security I felt as a child in the backseat of that car, knowing I could relax and leave my well-being in my father's hands. I wasn't afraid of getting lost because my dad knew every twist and turn in the road. I wasn't afraid of getting hurt because my father was big and strong and would stand up to anyone who might harm his family. And when we reached the end of our journey, I didn't even have to worry about being left out in the cold because my father was there to carry me safely home.

Thoughts to Ponder:

How does this parallel our heavenly Father's care?

In what ways are you resting in God's care?

Bumper Sticker for the Day:

> **Because of his love for us, every day should be Father's Day for God.**

Scripture to Stand On:

"Look at the birds of the air; they do not sow or reap or store away in barns, and yet your heavenly Father feeds them. Are you not much more valuable than they?"

MATTHEW 6:26

Hello Again, Lord ...

Lord, thank you for never leaving me out in the cold.

Sixty-nine

▲▼▲

Waiting to Change

Why is our youth leader making us pass out these tracts? Doesn't he know all my friends shop at this mall? What if I see someone from school? They're gonna think I'm some kind of religious geek or something.

Have you ever thought that? Have you ever found yourself wishing your youth pastor had scheduled a bowling night, or paint balling, or anything else except passing out tracts? They just end up in the trash anyway.

Or do they?

There's a minister here in Southern California who has quite a remarkable testimony. He was a drug addict, homeless and living in a park, when a young boy approached him one day and simply handed him a gospel tract. The boy left, totally unaware of the miracle that was about to take place. The man read the tract, then later gave his heart to the Lord. He got his life back together, went to Bible school, became an ordained minister, and is now the pastor of a large church with a worldwide television ministry.

How did all of this come about? Because of a six-week revival meeting? No. Because God sent an angel to appear to the man and convince him to change his ways? No. It all happened because of a little tract, the faithfulness of one young boy, and a God who likes to take our simple acts of faith and obedience and perform astounding miracles with them.

Thoughts to Ponder:

How do you think that boy's going to feel when he gets to heaven and sees the thousands of souls who have come to know the Lord because he cared enough to share Jesus with a stranger?

Is there something that you've done that might have similar eternal results?

Bumper Sticker for the Day:

Often our simplest acts of faith produce the greatest results.

Scripture to Stand On:

"For I have not come to call the righteous, but sinners."

MATTHEW 9:13

Hello Again, Lord ...

Lord, may I always be faithful in sharing your gospel. Who knows whose life you're waiting to change through me?

Seventy

▲ ▼ ▲

A Stitch in Time

My husband and I have a goose-down comforter. For years we had heard how cozy and comfortable they are—so we finally bought one. We love it.

A few weeks ago, though, I started noticing that every time I shook out the comforter, tiny white puffs of down would start flying all over the room. (These were different than the tiny gray dust bunnies that usually fly around the room.)

Examining the comforter, I located a tear at the foot of it, approximately two inches long. I don't know how it got there, although, our cat did look awfully guilty, and I don't recall her having that white beard before.

Not wanting to lose any more of the down filling, I got several safety pins and pinned up the hole. It isn't a permanent solution. Some down still escapes through the sides of the hole, and will continue to do so until I take the time to properly repair it. But I'm not that skilled with a needle and thread. (My home economics teacher used to make me wear a full body thimble.)

Discouragement is like a tear in our spirit. We can pin up the tear ourselves, providing some sort of temporary solution; but, just like the down in that comforter, our joy will continue to escape until we take that hurt to the Lord and have the damage properly repaired.

Thoughts to Ponder:

Is there a tear in your spirit? How did it get there?

What do you think happens when we give our hurts to Jesus?

Bumper Sticker for the Day:

> **Some wounds need heavenly stitches.**

Scripture to Stand On:

"Blessed are the poor in spirit, for theirs is the kingdom of heaven."

MATTHEW 5:3

Hello Again, Lord ...

Thank you, Lord, that when you repair my spirit, your work's guaranteed for eternity.

Seventy-one

▲ ▼ ▲

Blind Spot

The other day I was complaining that I couldn't find my glasses. They didn't have prescription lenses or anything. They cost less than ten bucks at a local pharmacy. But they do help me read small print on things like medicine bottles. Without some sort of magnifying assistance, "take two tablets every four hours" ends up looking like "tickle ten tigers elbows for Henry."

While I continued to search for the glasses (and grumble to everyone in the house), God reminded me of a young lady I had met only a few months before. Lindy (not her real name) had been diagnosed with a brain tumor. The tumor was slowly stealing her eyesight, and doctors had told her, without a miracle, within a few years she could be totally blind.

And there I was complaining that I couldn't find a pair of $6.98 glasses!

In spite of Lindy's diagnosis, she had one of the most positive outlooks on life I have ever witnessed. She was full of joy and laughter, and she appreciated to the fullest each and every scene that entered her field of vision.

She credited her incredible joy to two things: her faith in God, and something noted actress Jeannette Clift George had once said to her. Right in the middle of her crisis, when things looked bleakest, Jeannette had asked Lindy, "Are you having fun with the life God gave you?"

Throughout your life, you're sure to come face to face

with some pretty tough times. I hope and pray you don't, but the fact is, everyone has their own burdens to bear. Whether you choose to waste your days wallowing in self-pity or give your troubles to the Lord and have fun with the life he gave you is up to you.

After that little nudge from the Holy Spirit, I quit worrying about whether I should take two tablets or tickle tiger elbows. I began thanking God for my 20-25 vision, and a host of other blessings I'd forgotten about.

What blessings are you looking at today, but not really seeing?

Thoughts to Ponder:
Are you having fun with the life God gave you?

Name a problem you're focused on right now. What blessing can you focus on instead?

Bumper Sticker for the Day:

> **Always focusing on our problems blinds us to our blessings.**

Scripture to Stand On:
"He causes his sun to rise on the evil and the good, and sends rain on the righteous and the unrighteous."

MATTHEW 5:45

Hello Again, Lord ...
Lord, remind me to appreciate and enjoy the life and the many blessings you've given me.

Seventy-two

▲▼▲

Sleepless in Sacramento

While on a recent business trip, I lost almost a whole night's sleep, thanks to the people in the room next to me. They had their television set on all night. The sound wasn't blaring or anything like that, but it was coming through the walls just enough to keep me from fully relaxing and drifting off to sleep.

I watched as the clock radio on the table next to my bed ticked its way to one, then two, and finally four o'clock in the morning! I thought to myself, "Don't those people ever sleep?! How rude and inconsiderate can they be?"

Just as I started to reach for the telephone to call the desk clerk, I made an interesting and quite embarrassing discovery. The sound that had been keeping me awake wasn't coming from the room next door at all. It was coming from the clock radio in my room right next to my bed! Evidently, the people who had rented the room before me had left it on at a very low volume. All night long, while I lay there grumbling and complaining, I had the power to correct the problem myself and didn't even realize it!

How many things in life are like that clock radio? We grumble about how much something is annoying us, we whine and complain, and even blame it on those around us, when all the while the problem and its solution lie within ourselves.

Thoughts to Ponder:

Is there a problem keeping you awake at night? What is it and what positive action can you take to do something about it?

Why do you think some people would rather complain about their problems than do something about them?

Bumper Sticker for the Day:

> **Sometimes we toss and turn in our beds because we haven't tossed out our self-pity and turned our problems over to Jesus.**

Scripture to Stand On:

"Take my yoke upon you and learn from me, for I am gentle and humble in heart, and you will find rest for your souls."

MATTHEW 11:29

Hello Again, Lord ...

Lord, when it's in my power to do so, help me to do my part to positively change my circumstances.

Seventy-three

▲▼▲

Get Out the Tissue

Is there a song that makes you cry every time you hear it? I have a whole list. Growing up it was tearjerkers like "Dead Man's Curve," "Daddy, Don't You Walk So Fast," "Patches," and the theme song to "Gilligan's Island." (All right, I don't actually sob on that last one, but I do tear up.)

Today, it's "Butterfly Kisses" and anything on the country western stations. Country songs can get the tears flowing faster than one of my onion casseroles. I've even penned a few country tunes myself—heartbreaking songs like "I Lost My True Love in a Meatloaf Explosion." It's a catchy tune, but it has yet to make it to the top of the billboard charts.

One song, though, that can start my tears flowing faster than any other is Ray Boltz's "Thank You for Giving to the Lord." What a great song! Have you ever thought about those lyrics and asked yourself who you're going to thank when you get to heaven?

I know when I step through those pearly gates, I'm going to have to sing 158 verses of that song, which, with my voice, will make people wonder if they made it to the right place! But I'm going to sing it anyway.

The first verse would be for Jesus. I'd want to thank him for dying on a cross for me and for always being there whenever I needed a friend.

I'd sing the next verse to my parents, grandparents, my sister, Linda, and other family members who have gone on

159

before me. I'd thank them for always exhibiting our heavenly Father's unselfish love. I'd rush to find my cousins, aunts, uncles, and friends for the next verse. But the song wouldn't end there. I'd thank my pastors, youth pastors, and a variety of singers and songwriters who have greatly influenced my life and probably don't even know it.

Next, I'd ... well, as you can see, this can go on and on. All I can say is it's a good thing I've got eternity!

Thoughts to Ponder:

Make a list of some of the people you want to thank when you get to heaven:

Who might thank you in heaven?

Bumper Sticker for the Day:

Are you making an eternal difference in someone's life today?

Scripture to Stand On:

"Come, you who are blessed by my Father; take your inheritance, the kingdom prepared for you since the creation of the world."

MATTHEW 25:34

Hello Again, Lord ...

Thank you, Lord, that your love has everlasting rewards.

Seventy-four

▲▼▲

What a Letdown!

Have you ever let God down? You're eating lunch in the school cafeteria and someone tells an off-color joke. You laugh along with everyone else because you don't want to stand out.

You're with your friends and they start gossiping about someone else. You know it's wrong, but you listen anyway.

You feel God leading you to invite that boy who sits next to you in history class to church with you, but you talk yourself out of it. Later, you find out that someone else invited him to their church and he accepted. It's great that he's going to church, but God was urging you to invite him. Now once again you've let God down.

You're not alone. Peter let our Lord down, too. And what's worse, he did it after bragging that he, of all people, would never do such a thing. But Jesus gave Peter a healthy dose of reality.

"I'm telling you now, Peter," Jesus said, "before the rooster crows tomorrow morning, you will deny me three times."

Jesus was right. Peter did deny him three times. While the angry mob was leading Jesus to Golgotha, Peter swore that he didn't even *know* Jesus. In fact, all of Jesus' friends let him down that day.

None of us want to let Jesus down deliberately. We try our best not to, but so often we do. But you know what?

Amazing as it sounds, as Jesus hung on that cross that day, he forgave every one of his friends for failing him, even Peter. And if we ask, Jesus will forgive our failures, too.

Thoughts to Ponder:

Can you think of a time when you failed Jesus?

What should we do when we've failed the Lord?

Bumper Sticker for the Day:

> **Sometimes the hardest person to forgive is myself.**

Scripture to Stand On:

"I tell you the truth," Jesus answered, "this very night, before the rooster crows, you will disown me three times."

MATTHEW 26:34

Hello Again, Lord ...

Lord, forgive me for those times I've failed you, even though you've never once failed me.

Seventy-five

▲ ▼ ▲

Going the Distance

I'm a distance runner. The day I take up running will be a long time in the distance! Don't get me wrong. I admit there are plenty of benefits to running. It does wonders for your cardiovascular system and it helps build strong leg muscles. Running can even make you taller. The last time I ran four miles, it made me two inches taller. (Of course when the blisters healed, I went back to my original height.)

Yet despite all the positive results that running can produce, I still don't enjoy that kind of physical exertion. Perhaps it's the endurance factor that makes running so difficult. If we get tired swimming, all we have to do is get out of the pool. If we're exhausted playing basketball, we just signal the coach and he'll take us out of the game. But running is different. If we get tired running, we could be six miles from our starting point, so we've got to keep going if we ever want to make it home.

The Christian journey is like long distance running. It doesn't matter how much energy we start out with. It doesn't matter how much skill and determination we have. Speed doesn't even count. The only thing that really matters is whether we get tired and give up, or whether we keep going and ultimately make it over the finish line.

Thoughts to Ponder:

Why is God more concerned with our endurance than our speed?

What "exercises" can we do daily to build up our spiritual endurance?

Bumper Sticker for the Day:

> **If the Christian walk were the Olympics, what medal would you be taking home?**

Scripture to Stand On:

"All men will hate you because of me, but he who stands firm to the end will be saved."

MATTHEW 10:22

Hello Again, Lord ...

Lord, may I always schedule a daily workout with your Word.

Seventy-six

▲▼▲

Path of Least Resistance

When is it easiest to resist that hot fudge sundae that the zipper on our jeans is telling us we don't need? Is it after we walk into Baskin-Robbins and order it? Is it easier to walk away after we watch the clerk drop those three scoops of creamy vanilla ice cream into the tulip glass, pour rich, gooey hot fudge all over it, and add a tower of whipped cream, topped by the nuts and a cherry? Or is it easiest to resist those calories by walking on the other side of the street, not even looking in that direction?

When is it easiest to say no to those friends who we know are going to bring us down? Is it while we're hanging with them on a Friday night, doing everything they're doing even though we know we shouldn't? Or would it be easier to resist their draw if we'd think and pray about their destructive influence on our lives before we even walked out our door?

And what about paying our tithe? Which is easier—to pay it after we've watched three hours of the Home Shopping Network and spent the rest of the evening shopping at the mall, or is it easier to set God's portion aside as soon as we cash our checks?

No one ever said temptation would be easy to resist. But we don't have to give it an unfair advantage by positioning ourselves as close to it as possible.

Thoughts to Ponder:

Is there a temptation that you might be flirting with?

What steps can you take today to distance yourself a little more from that temptation?

Bumper Sticker for the Day:

Never tempt temptation.

Scripture to Stand On:

"Watch and pray so that you will not fall into temptation. The spirit is willing, but the body is weak."

MATTHEW 26:41

Hello Again, Lord ...

Lord, remind me that the sooner I overcome temptation, the harder it'll be for it to overcome me.

Seventy-seven
▲ ▼ ▲

Attention!

Have you ever been caught not paying attention? Your teacher asks what the capital of Arkansas is and you wake up from your daydream just in time to answer, "I'll have fries with that."

You're in the middle of watching your favorite television program when your little brother interrupts, asking if he can borrow your new white shirt to paint in. You nod and don't realize what you have agreed to until he brings it back looking tie-dyed.

Not paying attention can cause us trouble. If we don't pay attention to the rules of an audition, we could end up tap dancing while everyone else is reciting Shakespeare. If we don't pay attention to our bills, our telephone line will be disconnected while we're right in the middle of giving the correct answer for that radio contest. And if we don't pay attention, we could accidentally throw a beautiful sixty-yard pass ... to the wrong end of the football field.

It's good to pay attention. In Matthew 24, Jesus tells us to pay attention to the signs of his second coming. He tells us what the world will be like at that time, and urges us to keep watch so we're not caught off guard.

Why not take a moment today to read Matthew 24? See how many of the signs mentioned there are already taking place. Wars, famines, earthquakes, pestilences—heard about any of those lately?

No one but God knows the exact day and time when our Lord will return to earth, and the Bible does tell us to "occupy" until he comes. But seeing how closely today's news reports resemble this passage of Scripture, maybe it'd be a good idea for all of us to start paying a little more attention.

Thoughts to Ponder:

Why do you think Jesus wanted us know the signs of his coming?

Knowing that Jesus is coming soon, what should we be busy doing?

Bumper Sticker for the Day:

> ## Jesus is coming back ...
> ## so don't slack.

Scripture to Stand On:

"Therefore keep watch, because you do not know on what day your Lord will come."

MATTHEW 24:42

Hello Again, Lord ...

Lord, help me to stay ready 24-7—all the time, everyday.

Seventy-eight
▲▼▲

In Whom Do You Trust?

Do you realize how many times we place our lives in the hands of others?

We board an airplane and don't even look at who's piloting it. Sure, a voice will come over the P.A. eventually and introduce himself (or herself), but that's after we're already above the ground some twenty thousand feet. If he were to say, "This is your pilot, Barney, speaking. I don't know how to fly this big shiny thing, but I love you," what could we possibly do about it at that point?

We trust the amusement park worker to secure the safety rail on that roller coaster ride so we'll stay in our seats during those triple upside down loops, instead of flying out and joining the space shuttle crew.

We trust the cook at that fast-food restaurant to serve fresh burgers, and not some meat that's brown on both sides before it ever hits the grill.

We're a trusting people. We trust people with our lives and our health every day. So why do we have such a hard time trusting God? Maybe it's because it's easier to understand man's shortcomings than to comprehend God's infallibility. It still doesn't make much sense, though. After all, which is easier to do—trust the pilot or the One who rules the skies?

Thoughts to Ponder:

Have you ever had a difficult time trusting God? Tell about it:

Why is it always best to put our trust in our heavenly Father?

Bumper Sticker for the Day:

> ## Glasses and car keys aren't the easiest things to misplace. Trust is.

Scripture to Stand On:

When he had gone indoors, the blind men came to him, and he asked them, "Do you believe that I am able to do this?" "Yes, Lord," they replied.

MATTHEW 9:28

Hello Again, Lord ...

Lord, help me to keep my trust firmly planted in you.

Seventy-nine
▲▼▲

Follow the Leader

Did you know that God has a plan for your life? It might not be what you expect. I used to think I'd like to become a professional singer. I don't know why I thought that because I've never been able to carry a tune. (At my church, they've issued me the only choir robe that comes with a gag.) But a lot of my friends had dreams of becoming singers, so I dreamed it, too. To the relief of the music industry and the dismay of earplug manufacturers worldwide, God had a different plan for my life.

God's plan for your life might not be what others think it should be either. My mother gave me six years of piano lessons, hoping I'd become a concert pianist someday. Today the only thing I can do with a piano is dust it.

What I do love to do, though, is write. When I was nine years old, I wrote my first book, called *No Fun Being Young*. It was about being the youngest in a family of five children, and of course, it was never published (editors had a hard time reading crayon), but that experience started me on the path of what ended up being God's will for my life.

God has a plan for your life, too. It may be exactly the same as your plans, or it could be beyond your wildest dreams. One thing's for sure. You'll never know where it can lead unless you follow it.

Thoughts to Ponder:

Do you think you know what God's plan for your life is?

How can you know for sure that it's God's plan and not your own?

Bumper Sticker for the Day:

When we can have God's best, why
would we settle for less?

Scripture to Stand On:

"Then the righteous will shine like the sun in the kingdom of their Father."

MATTHEW 13:43

Hello Again, Lord ...

Lord, grant me the courage to be what you want me to be.

Eighty

▲▼▲

Lend Me an Ear

Ever get angry? Lose your temper? Act before you think? No doubt we all have on occasion.

Peter did, in the Garden of Gethsemane. When the soldiers were trying to take his Lord and friend, Peter reacted by drawing his sword and cutting off the ear of one of the high priest's servants. Jesus healed the man's ear because he knew what he was about to face was all in the plan of God. Peter didn't fully understand this, nor did he take the time to ask Jesus about it. He simply reacted.

That's the trouble with acting before we think, in the heat of the moment. We could be wrong, out of the will of the Lord, and it could take a miracle of God later to fix the mess our tempers have made.

That's not to say that it's always wrong to get angry. There are some things in life over which we should get upset. Even Jesus got angry at the money-changers in the temple. But the Bible does tell us not to sin in our anger. It also warns that uncontrolled, continuous anger can open us up to other problems in life. In Proverbs 25:28 we read, "Like a city whose walls are broken down is a man who lacks self-control."

So, if you find yourself flipping your lid a little too often, pray about it, get good counseling on anger management, and learn to count to ten before reacting to situations. Maybe even to twenty. After all, life is a lot less stressful if you leave the eruptions to the volcanoes.

Thoughts to Ponder:

Why do you think it's important that we think before we act?

Can you think of a time when you didn't think before you acted? Tell about it:

Bumper Sticker for the Day:

He who is quick to anger ...
is probably trying to program
his VCR.

Scripture to Stand On:

With that, one of Jesus' companions reached for his sword, drew it out and struck the servant of the high priest, cutting off his ear.

MATTHEW 26:51

Hello Again, Lord ...

Lord, remind me that blowing my top only leaves me looking like I've got a hole in my head.

Eighty-one

▲▼▲

Bookkeeping 101

Have you ever met someone who thought they had exclusive access to heaven's admission and reward records? They knew who was going to get in, and who was going to be turned away at the gate. They knew the precise size of everyone's mansion and crown. And they were certain of their accuracy because for years they'd been keeping their own set of books, just in case God missed anything.

What people like this don't realize is God doesn't have or need an earthly secretary. He alone knows someone's heart. Because of this, heaven is going to be one big surprise party. Some of the people we thought had no chance of admittance might be the very first ones to run up and welcome us, while others who we were certain would make it might be nowhere in sight.

It'll work the same way with the rewards. Those people we assumed would be wearing the biggest crowns might have theirs dwarfed by the one given that unassuming widow who faithfully taught Sunday school for forty years. And who knows what other surprises are in store for us?

One thing we can be sure of, though, is that God's a good bookkeeper. He doesn't need our help. We're supposed to do our best to point others to his light, show them the way and how the Bible says we are to live, but beyond that, we're stepping into his domain. In other words, he's the one who will make the final assessment of someone's eternal destiny. He's the only one qualified for that role.

Thoughts to Ponder:

Why do you think God is the best one to judge someone's life?

Do you think people who continually judge others have spent enough time assessing their own lives? Why or why not?

Bumper Sticker for the Day:

God's judgment seat
wasn't built for two.

Scripture to Stand On:

"For the Son of Man is going to come in his Father's glory with his angels, and then he will reward each person according to what he has done."

MATTHEW 16:27

Hello Again, Lord ...

Lord, remind me that your record books never need auditing.

Eighty-two
▲▼▲

Costume Party

What's the hottest fashion for wolves this season? According to the Bible, it's sheep's clothing. God warns us that there are a lot of wolves dressing up like sheep these days—false prophets, teachers, even friends who appear harmless, but are far from it.

So, how can we tell who's a wolf and who's a sheep? By keeping our eyes open and our defenses ready.

To spot a "pseudo-sheep," it's important to understand the species. Sheep have a pattern of behavior completely contrary to that of a wolf. Sheep follow shepherds. Wolves eat them.

Never trust a wolf. No matter how much he pretends to be as "gentle as a lamb," no matter what kind of costume he's wearing, he's still a wolf at heart. He's always looking out for his own best interests. He'll use trickery, intimidation, anything he has to in order to conquer his prey. It's who he is.

So don't be fooled by the wool. Be smart, and if you happen to run across a sheep that looks suspicious, forget his appearances. Check out how his actions line up with God's Word. Even underneath a convincing disguise, you should be able to tell whether that sheep has the heart of a lamb ... or the appetite of a wolf.

Thoughts to Ponder:

Have you ever been fooled by a "wolf" in sheep's clothing? What did you learn from the experience?

Which do you think is more dangerous—a wolf or a wolf in sheep's clothing? Why?

Bumper Sticker for the Day:

With some people we encounter, it's a True or False test.

Scripture to Stand On:

"Watch out for false prophets. They come to you in sheep's clothing, but inwardly they are ferocious wolves."

MATTHEW 7:15

Hello Again, Lord ...

Lord, as one of your flock, give me the peace to enjoy the pasture, but the wisdom to remember the wolves.

Eighty-three

▲ ▼ ▲

Curfews

Parents tend to worry until all their children are safely home at night. It's what we do. It doesn't matter if the rest of the family is already fast asleep in bed. We sit there on the sofa, watching every infomercial ever made. We order engine cleaner, car wax, juicers, skin care products (probably made out of the same ingredients as the engine cleaner), and we watch the clock. We wait and pray.

When my sons were young, their curfew was when the sun went down. They didn't always agree with this curfew. In fact, they probably would have loved growing up in Alaska, where the sun doesn't set for six months straight. Then they could have played outside for half a year before checking in. But our "in the house by sunset" rule sure helped me rest a lot easier.

Did you know God is equally protective of us? In Matthew 18, Jesus tells the parable of the lost sheep. It seems a certain shepherd could account for ninety-nine of his sheep, but one was nowhere to be found.

Now, most people wouldn't have blamed the shepherd had he simply left the missing sheep behind. After all, it was the sheep's own fault for wandering off. How many times had the shepherd sent him to obedience school? How often had he warned him of the dangers, the pitfalls, and the wolves? But that sheep didn't listen. He took off, and now there was no telling what kind of trouble he'd gotten himself into.

But the good shepherd didn't care that it was the sheep's

fault. He just wanted him home. He searched hillside after hillside, creek after creek. He may have even posted a few "missing sheep" posters around town. He kept looking and looking, and when he finally found him, the shepherd was so happy, he called all his friends and neighbors together and threw a big party!

Jesus paralleled the story of the lost sheep to God's love. He says that God wants all of his children safe within his fold, too. And when we finally come home to him, he rejoices just as much as that shepherd!

Thoughts to Ponder:

Why do you think that one lost sheep was so important to the shepherd?

If lost sheep are this precious to God, how important should they be to us?

Bumper Sticker for the Day:

> ### God's search party is never called off.

Scripture to Stand On:

"What do you think? If a man owns a hundred sheep, and one of them wanders away, will he not leave the ninety-nine on the hills and go to look for the one that wandered off? And if he finds it, I tell you the truth, he is happier about that one sheep than about the ninety-nine that did not wander off."

MATTHEW 18:12-13

Hello Again, Lord ...

Lord, help me to always stay within your fold, and to do my part to help others find their way home, too.

Eighty-four
▲▼▲

Let Sleeping Dogs Lie ...
(Especially If They Just Ate My Leftovers)

Have you ever startled a sleeping dog? Sleeping dogs don't like to be bothered. If they don't know you, you run the risk of getting bitten. Sometimes you run the risk of getting bitten even when they *do* know you.

Some of the issues that come up in our lives are like sleeping pit bulls. We're a lot better off leaving them alone. That doesn't mean these issues aren't important, or that we don't have the right to correct an injustice we've suffered. It just means that waking up that "sleeping dog" might cause us more of a problem than it's worth.

But how do we know which problems are the ones we should confront and which ones are the sleeping pit bulls? By praying and asking God for wisdom. We also should think ahead to the consequences of confronting or not confronting the issue. If confronting it is worth the consequences, and if God's leading us to confront it, then by all means, we should do it.

On the other hand, if we're merely wanting to confront it for our own fleshly desire to "put that person in their place" or "give them a piece of our mind," then we should probably leave that sleeping dog where it's safest—in God's hands.

Thoughts to Ponder:

Do you have a "sleeping dog" issue that you've decided to leave alone? Tell about it:

Why do you think it might be better to let this sleeping dog lie?

Bumper Sticker for the Day:

> **Whenever you feel like biting back, remember it's easier than you think to get more than you can chew.**

Scripture to Stand On:

"Blessed are the peacemakers, for they will be called sons of God."

MATTHEW 5:9

Hello Again, Lord...

Lord, help me to remember that when I leave a matter alone, I'm really just leaving it to you.

Eighty-five
▲▼▲

The Complaint Department

Benjamin Franklin once said, "He that's content has enough. He that complains has too much."

He was right. Most people who have little are usually thankful for what little they have. It's the people who have plenty, but who covet more, who usually complain.

Complainers are easy to recognize. Their lifestyles don't match their complaints. They complain about not having any clothes to wear, but do it in a different outfit everyday. They complain they don't have any money, but you've yet to see them on a corner holding a sign that says "Will work for brunch." When compared to the truly needy, these people are millionaires, but they still have to complain. They're not a very good testimony to God's goodness either.

There's a sign above my kitchen sink that says "Count your blessings." I try to do that every day. God is faithful and good. Sure, there are rough times that we all have to endure, times when we wish we could make our money stretch a little more. But to fool ourselves into thinking we have a right to complain when we're eating three meals a day, have a roof over our head, clothes to wear, and a warm bed to sleep in is ridiculous. If you don't think so, visit a homeless shelter sometime.

My son and his friends once wanted to see what it would be like to be homeless, so they took a loaf of bread and a bag of chips and set off, intent on spending the night out in the cold. About two o'clock in the morning, they came home shivering, hungry, and very thankful for what they had.

So, the next time you start to complain, think about all the things you have, instead of the few you don't have.

Thoughts to Ponder:

List some blessings in your life that you may have overlooked:

When you consider all you've been blessed with, do you think you have a right to complain? Why or why not?

Bumper Sticker for the Day:

> **When it comes to counting their blessings, a lot of people forget how to add.**

Scripture to Stand On:

"Therefore I tell you, do not worry about your life, what you will eat or drink; or about your body, what you will wear. Is not life more important than food, and the body more important than clothes?"

MATTHEW 6:25

Hello Again, Lord ...

Lord, forgive me for those times I've taken your blessings for granted, and failed to see how rich I am in you.

Eighty-six
▲▼▲

On the Right Track

A local amusement park has a ride where guests who meet the required height standards get to drive miniature cars along a miniature highway. It's a fun ride, and to a youngster who's not old enough for a regular driving license, it's the ultimate thrill. He or she can press the gas pedal all the way to the floor, turn the steering wheel in any direction, and stop in the middle of the road for no reason at all—with no fear of getting a ticket. Oh, there may be a few bumps along the way, an occasional eight-car pile-up, but the chances of truly getting hurt on this ride are pretty slim.

Why? Because the cars are on a track. The track will let the driver go just so far to the right or to the left before pulling them back. Parents, I'm sure, appreciate this track. It keeps their inexperienced child or preteen from driving over a bridge and landing in the shrubbery below.

If the amusement park wanted to, they could remove this track and let everyone drive however they pleased. It might be fun for awhile, but I have a feeling most of the cars would end up in the repair station.

The Holy Spirit is like that track. If we keep our lives connected to him, he lets us know when we're veering off too far away from safety, or when we're headed in the wrong direction. We can take our lives off his track and live however we want to, but then we might end up having to spend most of our time in the repair station, too.

Thoughts to Ponder:

Tell of a time when the Holy Spirit nudged you back on track:

Why do you think it's to our benefit to allow the Holy Spirit to keep us from getting off track?

Bumper Sticker for the Day:

> **It doesn't matter if we're making excellent time if we're driving in the wrong direction.**

Scripture to Stand On:

"Be perfect, therefore, as your heavenly Father is perfect."

MATTHEW 5:48

Hello Again, Lord ...

Lord, thank you for the Holy Spirit's gentle nudging. May he never need a megaphone to get my attention.

Eighty-seven
▲▼▲

Making Memories

Is there a relationship in your life you'd like to improve? Perhaps you're wishing you and your mother could be closer. Maybe you'd like your father to spend more time with you. Whoever it is you're longing to have a better relationship with, don't simply wait for it to happen. *Make it happen.*

Too many people go through their lives wishing things could change. They know what they want to happen, they complain that it hasn't happened, but they do very little to change the situation themselves.

If you'd like to be able to spend more time with your mother, then plan a special outing for just the two of you. Chances are, she'll be delighted. If she's too busy this week, then plan it for next week. Or the next. *But do it.*

If you find yourself wishing you and your dad could do more activities together, don't just tell him that. Ask him for an available date and schedule a father-son or father-daughter day. If he lets you down, don't give up. Schedule another one. They're your memories. Make them what you want them to be.

Feeling sad because none of your friends have called you lately? Don't sit idly by waiting for the telephone to ring. Call them. Or call a new friend—maybe that boy or girl who visited youth group last week. All too often the only thing that's keeping a relationship from improving is someone taking the initiative to make it happen.

Life is what we make it, and it's too short to simply wait for good times to come our way. Sometimes we have to give them a nudge. The sun hasn't stood still since Joshua fought the Amorites. We'll never have this particular day again, so we should use it to the fullest. After all, when we get to the end of our life, there isn't a prize for the person with the most disappointments. So, why do we go on collecting them?

Thoughts to Ponder:

What relationship would you like to improve?

What steps can you take today to start improving that relationship?

Bumper Sticker for the Day:

> **Relationships are like a bank account. If we never put anything into them, we'll always come up short.**

Scripture to Stand On:

"If someone forces you to go one mile, go with him two miles."

MATTHEW 5:41

Hello Again, Lord ...

Lord, instead of merely complaining about my relationships, help me to do my part to improve them.

Eighty-eight
▲▼▲

Sticks and Stones

Most adults clearly remember the nicknames they were called as children—so much for the old "sticks and stones may break my bones, but names will never hurt me" myth.

In high school my nickname was Olive Oyl. I was tall and thin, so the other kids at school figured it was a natural. Actually, I didn't really mind the nickname. It was a whole lot better than the cruel names some of the other kids had to endure.

That was one thing about Jesus—he always stood up for those being put down by others; the underdog; the downtrodden; those men, women, teenagers, and children who couldn't stand up for themselves. Jesus was on their side. He wasn't afraid to confront the "bullies" of his day and defend the victims.

From Mary Magdelene to Zacchaeus the tax collector, Jesus wasn't afraid to be their friend, to forgive and encourage them, to call them by their names, not what others had called them. As his followers, we should do nothing less.

Thoughts to Ponder:

Do you know someone who's had to endure name-calling? How do you think it makes them feel?

Do you add to this person's pain by joining in the name-calling or do you try to stop it?

Bumper Sticker for the Day:

What's in a name?
Kindness or pain.

Scripture to Stand On:

"The good man brings good things out of the good stored up in him, and the evil man brings evil things out of the evil stored up in him."

MATTHEW 12:35

Hello Again, Lord ...

Lord, may the words I say to people today lift them up, not tear them down.

Eighty-nine
▲▼▲

Return Trips

When I was young, one of my favorite things to do was to climb up a tree in our backyard, then jump onto the roof of our garage. It was about a three-foot span, and I always made it with ease. Jumping back to the tree was a little trickier. That leap usually landed me face down in the dirt below.

Those mishaps, with all the scrapes and bruises, taught me something very important about return trips. They're not always as easy as they look.

Throughout our lives we might be tempted to jump away from God. It seems easy enough. We'll just take a short leap, do our own thing for awhile, then jump right back into his waiting arms. What we're not considering, though, is what we may have to go through before we make it back. We could have to suffer some nasty emotional scrapes and bruises, perhaps even fall on our faces a few times.

But just like that tree, God didn't move out from under us. We were the ones who left. He's still where he's always been, standing with arms outstretched toward us, ever ready to welcome us back, no matter how much dirt and mud we've gotten all over ourselves. It's comforting to know that, but then again, why would anyone want to leave him in the first place?

Thoughts to Ponder:

Have you ever had to make a "return trip" to God?

What made you leave him? Was it worth it? Why not?

Bumper Sticker for the Day:

God created our backs,
but he never intended to see
them turned toward him.

Scripture to Stand On:

Then Peter remembered the word Jesus had spoken: "Before the rooster crows, you will disown me three times." And he went outside and wept bitterly.

MATTHEW 26:75

Hello Again, Lord ...

Lord, may I never take your love and forgiveness for granted.

Ninety
▲▼▲

The Ultimate Biography

There's a popular television show called *Biography*. Each episode profiles a different person, living or dead, who has left a mark on society. The greatness of all those men and women combined, though, will never compare to this man:

He was born in a stable in Bethlehem and was confounding temple scholars by the time he was twelve.

Though royalty, he never demanded special treatment. No one rolled out the red carpet for him to walk on, but he did walk on water.

Only one parade was ever held in his honor, but a week later the cheering crowd led him down the very same street to crucify him.

They didn't give him an Oscar, an Emmy, or a Grammy, but they did give him a crown of thorns.

He wasn't valedictorian of his class, but he was victor over death, hell, and the grave.

He didn't win the Nobel Peace Prize, but he is the Prince of Peace.

You won't find his face on the cover of weekly news magazines, even though the book written about him is still the biggest seller in history.

He is, without a doubt, the most quoted person in history, and his presence in this world has indeed made it a better place.

He's not the Man of the Hour, the Man of the Year, or the Man of the Century. He's the Man of Eternity.

He never ran for senator, governor, or president, but he's King of Kings and Lord of Lords.

His name is Jesus.

Thoughts to Ponder:

Why do you think Jesus' life made such an impact on the world?

If you were asked in an interview what Jesus means to you, what would you say?

Bumper Sticker for the Day:

> **Jesus—the greatest man who ever lived, died, and lived again.**

Scripture to Stand On:

"Therefore go and make disciples of all nations, baptizing them in the name of the Father and of the Son and of the Holy Spirit, and teaching them to obey everything I have commanded you. And surely I am with you always, to the very end of the age."

MATTHEW 28:19-20

Hello Again, Lord ...

Lord, thank you for who you are, and for loving me unconditionally.